BOWLER'S HANDBOOK

A Guide to [almost] Everything in Bowling

Ron McIntosh

McIntosh Publishing, Inc. Elfers, Florida

ISBN: 1-4276-0496-7

Contents

INTRODUCTION

Bowler's Handbook: A Guide to (almost) Everything in Bowling is written and designed to be a reference to the important elements in the sport of bowling for beginners and veterans alike.

While we begin this handbook with bowling lessons from some of the best amateur bowlers in the United States, we urge readers to first look at the sections about bowling courtesy, equipment and getting ready to bowl because bowlers should be physically ready to bowl, know what equipment is needed and have a firm understanding of the basic manners expected in the sport.

In the bowling lesson section readers will meet many of the sport's amateur record holders who willingly share their knowledge of bowling and some of the mental gyrations and adjustments they had to make while setting bowling records.

Karen Rosenburg, Rolla, Mo., talks about her record 878 series and what she does to consistently hit high scores and average more than 210 over the past 18 years. She also talks about the night of the record, and why being tired that night was a big help.

Darin Baginski, 31-year-old from New Port Richey, Fla., who has recorded 39 perfect games and 22 three-game 800 totals, is not only a great bowler, he is also a great student of the game. He, too, shares his bowling insight.

Dean Wolf, a chiropractor from Reading, Pa., who has registered 75 perfect games and 46 three-game 800 totals, discusses his methods and how he handles the jitters that come with big time scores.

Ed Duer, 71-year-old New Port Richey, Fla., retiree explains his "simple" bowling style. He has 52 sanctioned 300 games, 34 of which came after his 60th birthday.

Kristen Yeagley, 36-year-old mother who began bowling at the age of 6, set the all-time average record for women on a five-member team in 2004-2005 with a 230 average in her Lebanon, Pa., bowling league. She posted a 228 in 2003-2004 and repeated the 230 average in 2005-2006 for a three-year average of 229.3. She carefully and clearly talks about her bowling skills and how she maintains her outstanding high scoring consistency.

Jeff K. Campbell II talks about the night he became just the sixth person in bowling history to record a perfect 900 series.

All of bowling's greatest records are listed here, as are the methods of scoring, averaging and handicapping, major rules, history, strategies and the sport's distinctive vernacular.

There also are sections on exercising and stretching before bowling and how to figure out lane conditions, plus much more.

Bowler's Handbook does not overload readers with unimportant data and obscure theories, but presents clear, concise and easy-to-find information on almost everything a bowler needs to know or wants to know about America's favorite participant sport.

We hope you enjoy this book, tell others about it, and always hit the pocket. -- Ron McIntosh

Fast Facts

Frank Clause, Old Forge, Pa., won $67,000 in two TV bowling shows in the early 1960s. After that success, the high school English and history teacher traveled the world as an AMF representative. Clause authored two bowling books and wrote a syndicated bowling column. Born in 1913, he died in 1977. Throughout his career he registered 11 sanctioned 300 games. He was inducted into the Bowling Hall of Fame in 1980.

FRANK CLAUSE, left, bowling for a publicity photo at Riverside Lanes in Susquehanna, Pa., in 1965 with local bowling star Bob Furkay. *(William S. Young photo)*

BOWLING LESSONS FROM THE BEST

In this section nine of the best amateur bowlers in the United States share their knowledge of key components in the sport of bowling. Each bowler, starting with 230+ average bowler **Darin Baginski**, was interviewed and asked to discuss bowling techniques and offer advice to other bowlers.

The bowlers explain how they hit the big scores and why they use the techniques they use. *(The author believes that when we understand why something is done it makes the how of that action much more understandable.)* In each bowler section, and in the following summary (In a Nutshell) section bowling technique is examined part by part, including approach, aim, loft, timing, release, ball rotation, follow through, striking strikes, throwing hook balls, practice and the mental game.

Together, the amateur bowlers in this *Bowling Lessons from the Best* section have registered 96 three-game 800 totals, 190 perfect games, and have a combined average of more than 220. Two of the bowlers -- **Karen Rosenburg** with the women's all-time best three-game total of 878 and **Jeff K. Campbell II** with a 900 series -- hold national and state records.

A brief biographic sketch of each bowler is presented, followed by the bowler's discussion on how and why he or she handles the many aspects and techniques of bowling. Common bowling faults are discussed and outlined following each bowler's advice section.

Featured in this section are:

***Darin Baginski** , New Port Richey, Fla., averages more than 230, has recorded 39 perfect games and 22 three-game 800 totals. He is only 31 years old. (Page 5)

***Karen Rosenburg**, Rolla, Mo., bowler whose 878 three games series of 299, 279, 300 is the best ever posted by a women in bowling history. (Page 24)

***Kristen Yeagley**, 36-year-old mother of two who began bowling' at the age of 6, set the all-time average record for women on a five-member team in 2004-2005 when she recorded a 230 in Lebanon, Pa. She also recorded a 230 average in 2005-2006. (Page 11)

***Ed Duer**, 71-year-old New Port Richey, Fla., bowler has recorded

51 perfect games, 34 since the age of 60. He has averaged more than 220 for 20 years. (Page 27)

Mike Allen, 42-year-old New Port Richey, Fla., bowler averages more than 210 in four leagues and rolled back-to-back 300 games in 2005 in different bowling centers. (Page 16)

Dean Wolf, Reading, Pa., bowler has 75 perfect games, 46 800 series and an 898 three-game total that because of a mechanical breakdown was bowled on two sets of lanes. His 75 perfect games ranks him second all-time in that category. (Page 19)

Bob Blechner is a 64-year-old semiretired New York City bank officer who moved to Bayonet Point, Fla., and found more time to bowl. In the past four years he has averaged more than 200 with a 222 season in 2003 and a 217 in 2004 that included a sanctioned 300 game. (Pg. 32)

Kevin McManus, a candlepin bowler from Massachusetts, began 10-pin bowling when he moved to Florida in 1995. He registered a 213 season average in 2003-2004 and has four sanctioned 300 games. He is a USBC silver level bowling coach. (Page 10)

Jeff K. Campbell II recorded a 900 series June 12, 2004, in New Castle, Pa. It was the sixth perfect series recorded in the history of bowling. Campbell, who averages more than 230, came close to a second 900 series March 30, 2006, when he hit 34 strikes in an 869 series in Amarillo, Texas. (Page 34)

Following the individual section is a compendium summary section (Page 39) (*Help in a Nutshell*) that includes an overview of each element of bowling, the main ideas offered by our top bowlers on those elements. A more detailed analysis of release positions (Page 51) and loft (Page 52) concludes this section of *Bowling Lessons from the Best*.

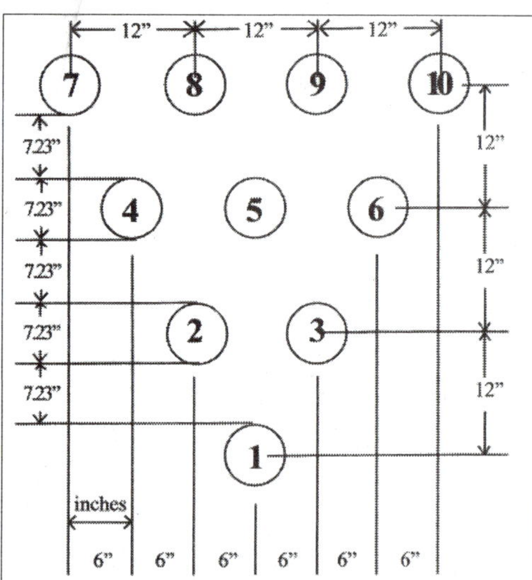

How easy is it to hit a pin? A bowling ball is nearly nine inches wide and pins are 4.77 inches wide at their broadest point 4.5 inches up from the base.

Darin Baginski

DARIN BAGINSKI, an amateur bowler who enjoys that status and has no intentions of turning professional, is on his way to becoming one of bowling's foremost record holders. The 31-year-old's bowling credentials already include 22 sanctioned 800 series, 39 sanctioned 300 games, six 299s and four 298s. In the past three years the New Port Richey, Fla., resident has averaged more than 230 in two leagues, including a 237 in 2003-2004 that was the best in Florida's Suncoast Bowling Association. A native of Westerville, Ohio, a city of 30,269 in the center of the state near Columbus, Baginski has been bowling since he was 10 years old. Although he is chief mechanic for Lane Glo Lanes in New Port Richey, he practices just three or four games a week and relies on his league bowling and tournament bowling to keep sharp. "When I was 16 and 17 years old and trying to really improve I bowled at least 100 games a week every week for a year and a half. The local lanes had a special of three hours for $5 and I took advantage of that"

Mental Game -- "I just take one ball at a time. If it is league bowling I take it serious, but not as serious as tournament bowling. I have the same routine every time. I get up there, dry my hands, wipe my ball off and think about throwing a strike."

> # DARIN BAGINSKI
>
> •31 Years Old
> •39 Perfect Games
> •22 800s
> •Averages 230+

Suppose you are having a bad night. How do you change it? "I try to find something new. I move my target. I throw a different bowling ball, something that reacts a little different, maybe less hook or maybe a little more hook. I try to think positive and tell myself to 'come on, throw a good ball.' I try not to worry about what I did last frame, especially if I had an open."

•Trouble Spot: Bowlers get far too involved in their scores. How many times have you seen a bowler throw two good games, then collapse in the last game because he or she applies so much pressure they tense up or change their style in an attempt to shoot a certain score.

Approach -- "I try to get relaxed on the approach, with the ball and everything. I take a good look at my mark on the lane and get my feet lined up on my spots. Sometimes I shake a little bit to help me relax. Then I just take my five steps and go. Five steps helps me get a little more ball speed than I do with four steps. The key is to put your ball in the same place all the time for the strike shots, and move your starting point -- where you place your feet -- to adjust to the lane. Remember, you don't want to play where you want to play, you want to play where the lane wants you to play."

•Trouble Spot: Inconsistency is a bowler's biggest enemy. When you are on the approach, find a style that works for you and stick to it each time. Even consistent bad styles are better than inconsistency. Stand in the same place and walk straight to the foul line. If you stand in a different place each time, wander on the approach left to right or change your speed and number of steps you take, it becomes impossible to develop a sound pattern.

Aim -- Baginski looks at the target from the time he gets set on the approach until the ball is released and passes over his target. "If I take my eye off the target before I release the ball," he said, " I will throw a bad ball. I try to concentrate on my target the whole time, all the way down the approach. I look up to see the path of the ball only after the ball has crossed over my target." Baginski targets an area rather than a specific board, dot or arrow. "I look for an area in the heaviest oil, usually between the second and third arrow, because if you play in the oil -- most of the oil on most lanes is across the lane from the second arrow to the second arrow -- you have some margin for error to the left and to the right."

•Trouble Spot: Low scoring bowlers don't always select a target, and those who do often have difficulty hitting it consistently for a variety of reasons, the usual reason for missing is simply not staying focused on the target. Again, find a target that looks lined up with the pins you want to hit and try to hit it. Remember, if your target -- such as a dot on the lane -- is closer to where you release the ball, you have a much better chance of hitting it than if it is a pin 60 feet away.

Loft -- "The loft should be a foot to three feet past the foul line depending on where you finish your slide or plant. I plant my left foot about three to four inches from the line, so my loft is about a foot. The more loft you have, the later the ball will hook down the lane. With more loft you make the lane shorter and delay your hook."

Trouble Spot: Rather than loft the ball -- or get it out on the lane -- many bowlers drop the ball or place the ball behind the foul lane, which in effect creates a longer lane and allows the ball to lose its drive before it reaches the pins. Lack of loft is often the result of being on top of the ball rather than under it when the ball is released. The other extreme is throwing the ball too far out on the lane or too high above the release point. (Note: Many bowling establishments will not permit high lofts because of the damage balls cause when they hit the lanes.)

Timing -- "Timing is the most important aspect of bowling. You should be releasing the ball at precisely the same time your slide or plant is ended. If you can do that, you can hit your target with a maximum of action on your ball. If you start the ball too early, your body will be ahead of the ball at the foul line and you will pull the ball. If your body is too far behind the ball, you will try to hurry and then you most often miss the shot. I don't slid, I just plant my foot, and I think that helps me with my timing." *Are you concerned that eventually you will hurt your knee?* "I haven't hurt my knee yet, but I do know that is a risk I take." Baginski's approach is not fast, so he does not plant abruptly, instead he comes to a smooth stop.

Trouble Spot: Very few athletes have natural timing. For the vast majority, timing is achieved and improved only with practice. Some people attempt to achieve better timing by singing a song, reciting a poem or counting movements as they complete their moving objective. Timing is usually the difference between a good night and a bad one.

Release -- "Keep your ball release as close to your body as you can without hitting your leg or your ankle. When I start my approach I just let my arm fall naturally with the ball. I just kind of drop it and let my arm go into a natural back swing. I don't force it. Keep your elbow in. Throughout the approach and release I keep my hand under the ball and my wrist flat. I get my thumb out of the ball first so I can feel the ball coming off my fingers." Baginski says a key to good scoring is consistently keeping your arm in close to your body and releasing the ball precisely when you finish your slide or plant the slide foot. He does not try to squeeze the ball during his release because "that leads to an early hook and a weak finish."

Trouble Spot: The actual release of the ball is the downfall of many bowlers. Many bowlers have floppy or weak wrists that rob them of the ability to rotate the ball properly. Some bowlers try to generate a hook or curve by turning their wrists. That extra movement causes all kinds of problems that include inconsistency, overturn and weak ball finish, and poor ball control. Backup balls -- also called reverse curves -- are caused by turning the wrist to the right for right handed bowlers, and turning the wrist to the left for left-handed bowlers. Backup balls hit the pins with less action than balls rotating naturally toward the pins so they simply do not score well.

Ball Rotation -- "I try to release the ball so it will roll on a right-to-left rotation of about 45 degrees through the oil into the dry area of the lane. The ball should skid through the oil -- some 37 to 40 feet -- and pick up momentum in the last 15 to 20 feet of the lane where it is dry. My fingers rotate the ball when I release it with a good follow through."

Follow Through -- "If you cut the follow through short, or have no follow through, the ball probably will hook early and have no finish, or no drive when it hits the pins. I try to have my hand hit the left side of my head a little bit after I follow through the ball. Some people can get away with a short follow through, but generally good follow throughs and good bowlers go together. Have you ever

seen a pro without a good follow through." Baginski says some bowlers follow through way to the left or right side, rather than up, in an attempt to get more hook on the ball. He does not recommend it because in any follow through other than toward the target and up requires perfect timing to achieve consistency. There is little room for error. "Some bowlers do that because they think more hook means more score. That's not true. More hook is less score."

Trouble Spot: The correct follow through is toward the bowler's target and up. A number of bowlers simply drop the ball and abruptly stop the forward motion of their hand at that point rather than continuing through with the ball hand. Follow through imparts rotation on the ball, and rotation translates into ball hitting power.

Stringing Strikes -- "Some people can't string strikes because as soon as they throw a couple they start thinking about it too much. I play one ball at a time, and try not to think about a string. I don't look at the score board, and I might not even think about bowling until I get on the approach. I might tell myself it is just practice, or I think about being consistent and about hitting the target. The biggest thing about pressure for me is throwing the ball too fast or too slow. I sometimes have a tendency to throw the ball too slow under pressure, so I tell myself to throw a good speed." *Is ball speed important?* "Yes. It is important in terms of consistency. If you throw too hard or too slow you can lose some of your timing and consistency. A ball thrown too hard might miss the head pin because it went down the lane too fast to catch the break point. I throw around 16 miles per hour, but speed doesn't really matter as long as you throw consistently."

Hook Ball -- How do you throw a hook ball? "A lot depends on the kind of ball. I like a resin ball. To hook the ball you have to get your thumb out of the ball first when you release it, then lift with your fingers so they rotate around the ball. The ball rotates sideways, horizontally down the lane through the oil. When the ball hits the dry area, anywhere from 10 to 15 feet in front of the pins, the ball will grab and hook in the direction of the ball rotation. You have to stay behind the ball, keep your wrist firm, and follow through when the ball is released. I think it also helps to have good finger inserts. They let you get more fingers into the ball with more cushion and more lift than the hard-hole ball. Your fingers need to be snug, and into the ball to the first knuckle. Keep them stiff at release."

Trouble Spot: Many bowlers attempt to hook the ball by rapidly rotating their wrists and the ball during the release. That movement will, to some degree, impart side rotation on the ball and some hook. The rapid movement of the wrist, however, also makes it difficult to maintain consistency, and over a period of time will cause some wrist soreness and damage.

Practice -- "Work on one thing at a time. Don't worry about your practice scores because in practice the scores don't mean anything. Always work on your timing."

Trouble Spot: Bowling a lot without a purpose is not the path to better bowling. Good bowlers have a purpose in their practice efforts such as working on particular spares, developing better timing, improving the release and so on. Good bowlers also seek help from bowling coaches and better bowlers. Repetition of a bad habit only makes it more difficult to get rid of that bad habit. Beginning bowlers who want to advance should seek coaching as soon as possible because it is much easier to simply learn the right way rather than erase bad habits.

Fast Facts

Bowling trick-shot artist **Andy Varipapa**, 1891-1984, won consecutive all-star match game titles in 1947 and 1948 at ages 52 and 53.

Kevin McManus

KEVIN McMANUS, New Port Richey, Fla, is a United States Bowling Congress silver-level bowling coach and a director of the Suncoast Bowling Association, Inc. He compiled a 213 season average in 2003-2004 at Lane Glo Lanes in New Port Richey. He has four sanctioned 300 games. Originally from Hull, Mass., McManus began bowling candlepins and only started bowling 10 pins after he moved to Florida in 1995.

Practice Ball -- "Bowlers always get a period for practice before league bowling begins. Use the time wisely." McManus says "throw a couple balls just to loosen up, then take a shot at a 7 pin, a 10 pin, a 6 and 4. When you do that you not only get ready for spares, you can find out how much oil is on the lane by checking the action of your ball. Does it slide, or does it grab? If the oil is heavy, you should get your ball on the lane earlier by picking a spot target closer to the foul line. If the oil is light, I pick a target further out on the lane and get the ball out more."

KEVIN McMANUS
*USBC Bowling Coach
*200+ Average
*Four 300s.

•Trouble Spot: In most centers bowlers take turns during the practice session, with one shooting at a full rack and the next shooting at whatever was left by the previous bowler. Forget the pins and shoot for the spares that will give you the best practice. Average time for pre-league practice shots is about 10 minutes, so don't waste that time or the time others have by not being ready when it is your turn, and taking too long on the lane. Bowling etiquette usually calls for each team member to take turns throwing a single shot, although some leagues follow a two-shot pattern for each bowler in turn. If you arrive late, you miss the chance to practice.

Kristen Yeagley

KRISTEN YEAGLEY,

36-year-old mother from Lebanon, Pa., has the second, third and fourth best all-time highest averages ever posted by a women in a five-member team league. In 2004-2005 and again in 2005-2006 she recorded a season average of 230 in the Thursday night 16-team Cedarette Handicap Women's League at Cedar Lanes in Lebanon. She also posted a 228 average in the same league in 2003-2004 to share the fourth best average with Paulette Karwoski (1982-1983) and Aleta Sill (Dearborn, Michigan, 1987-1988). Bonny Reed-Ball, bowling in the JBA Trucking League at Park Centre Lanes in Canton, Ohio, set the all-time high average record for women on five-member teams when she recorded a 232.6 in 2004-2005.

How does Yeagley, a right-handed bowler who has averaged 229 over the past three years and who has posted three 800s and three perfect games in her career, remain so consistent?

"I feel very comfortable bowling that night. It is the one night of the week I have to myself. I have bowled in the same league for 15 years. I bowl with my Mom and three friends. It is a really comfortable, relaxing night, and I go there trying to do my best for the team."

> # KRISTEN YEAGLEY
>
> *Second highest all-time average leader in five-member women's leagues with two 230s.
> *Three 800 totals.
> *Three 300 games.

Yeagley recorded a 225 average in the same bowling center in 2004-2005 in the three-member Friday night scratch league bowling with her husband, William.

Yeagley's parents introduced her to bowling at the age of seven. She participated in Lebanon's junior bowling program and attended five, week-long summer bowling programs conducted at Pennsylvania State University by the college's bowling coach and team. "It was a very good instructional program," Yeagley says. "They really broke the game down for me, videotaped me and gave me the basics."   Yeagley credits the junior bowling program and her husband with helping her learn hand positions and more advanced techniques.

Yeagley's junior girls team won a Pennsylvania state scratch championship and was ranked among the top 10 teams in the U.S. She went to nearby Kutztown University in Kutztown, Pa., on a basketball scholarship, but after a year and some injuries she quit basketball to focus more on academics. It was at that time she began bowling in the adult leagues in Lebanon."

Averaging more than 200 for the past 10 years, Yeagley bowls in a number of tournaments, and has been a member of the Women's All-Star Association (WASA) since 1996. She had one of her three 300 games in a WASA tournament in Maryland. In 2005 she hit her highest three-game total, an 827 in the Lebanon County Women's Tournament doubles event that also included a 300 game. During that same tournament she and her partner, Jodi Reppert, recorded a 1547 total, the fourth highest team series ever posted by two women. Their team game 567 (300 and 267) and series total was second best in the nation that year. Yeagley's nine-game all-events total of 2,254 was fourth best in the nation.

Yeagley was inducted into the Lebanon County Bowling Hall of Fame in 1998. She and her husband have a five-year old son and are expecting a second child in November, 2006.

PRACTICE (Warm-up) -- She does not have a lot of time for practice. "I don't walk in the door (of the bowling center) except to bowl on Thursday and Friday nights," Yeagley says. But she does compliment her regular bowling schedule with tournaments once a month and once a week summer league bowling. She does do some warm-up moves and has a routine to help her get ready for league bowling.

"I pick up the bowling ball and swing it around a little, trying to stretch my arms and loosen my back before actually throwing a ball," she says. "I also do some bending and get my mind set on bowling." Yeagley says she usually throws her most comfortable shot first, a ball over the second arrow. "I adjust from there. If it is not coming up into the pocket and I did everything right -- came through the ball well, had my feet right, threw a good shot -- then I know I have to adjust to the right or move back on the approach," she says. "If the ball came in high I know I have to move left or up, and tinker with it from there."

INSTRUCTION -- "I scan the magazines when they come in, especially the gold and bronze tips (featured in the *US Bowler* magazine), and try to watch professional bowling Sundays on television." (*Note: A complete list of bowling books, periodicals and videos is featured in the back of Bowler's Handbook.*)

APPROACH -- "I use a four-step approach, starting with the ball about waist high. I try to make sure I push the ball away on my first step, and that I don't go too high on my back swing."   Yeagley does not think about her foot speed, but rather is "trying to remember to stay down at the line, bend my knees and reach out across the lanes." "If I push the ball away correctly, that usually keeps my foot speed in check."

Trouble Spot: Most bowlers use a four- or five-step approach. A few use more steps, and some use as few as three. The trick is to make sure your approach matches your style in that you arrive at the foul line balanced and ready to release the ball. Many bowlers measure their steps by going to the foul line and walking along the approach to a starting point. Setting up your steps and spacing will help you avoid fouls.

BACK SWING -- "You need to have a controlled back swing," Yeagley says. "More power is not always necessarily better." She says she was taught and believes that the starting position height of the ball should be about equal to the height of the back swing. She also emphasizes that a good back swing should be a fluid, pendulum-like motion along the right side of the body for a right-handed bowler. "I try to make sure I keep the ball and the back swing controlled, and that I am not opening my shoulder, that the ball is coming straight back and not behind my back."

Trouble Spot: While the height of back swings vary from bowler to bowler, the one constant is that the back swing should be the major determinant in ball speed.   A high back swing should bring more ball speed.

ELBOW -- "The elbow is a key for me," Yeagley said. "I think it is important to lock the elbow on the back swing and keep it locked through

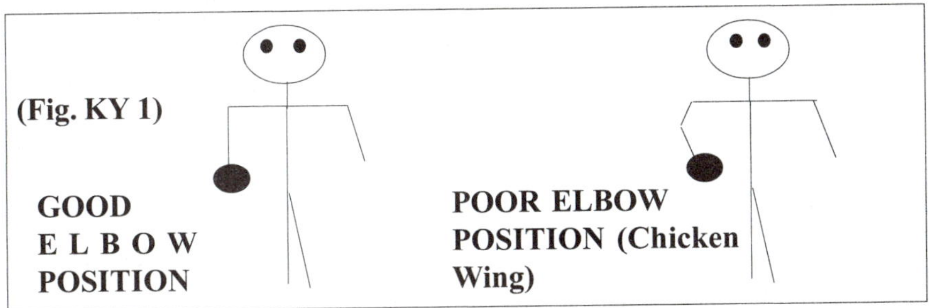

the forward swing to avoid 'chicken winging' the ball." (*See Fig. KY1*)

RELEASE -- "My husband always tells me I need to remember to accelerate through the shots and not decelerate," Yeagley says about her ball release at the line. "I also try to make sure I keep my hand behind the ball as I come through with it and then rotate it as I come out of it. Occasionally I catch myself coming around the ball, and I have to watch that. You have to stay behind the ball."

Her thumb position is at about 9 o'clock in her start position, rotated to 12 o'clock in her back swing, and back to 9 o'clock in her release. She maintains a flat wrist.

BALL ROTATION -- Yeagley throws a full, or high roller with a flare (ball track) of about two inches.

TARGET -- Yeagley throws a strong, down-and-in hook ball. On occasion, when conditions call for it, she also throws a curve that can cover from five to seven boards. "I usually stand at the second set of dots and line up my left foot with the center dot," she says. "I walk straight to my mark, which is usually the second arrow." She hits her mark at least eight out of 10 times.

BOWLING BALL -- "I was taught that you get a bowling ball and have it drilled to do the work for you," Yeagley says. "If you try to force the ball, then you are not letting the ball do the work, and you can't be consistent. So I try to make sure I have the mechanics right, stay behind the ball, follow through, hit my mark, and let the ball hook or not hook depending on what I want it to do."

Yeagley throws a 16-pound ball with a finger tip grip. She carries six different balls to tournaments, including a plastic ball she uses to shoot straight at her right-side spares. She throws her strike ball for spares on the left side.

LOFT -- "I try to make sure I get the ball out, that I reach out," she says. Yeagley does not loft the ball as in throwing it higher than her release point, but throws it long (about six feet out) and low on the lane. "A number of people tell me that they do not hear the ball when I place it on the lane."

FOLLOW THROUGH -- "The follow through is the execution," Yeagley says. "You can have everything else correct -- the timing, the speed -- but if you don't execute the follow through, you will not get the results you need." When Yeagley completes her follow through her right hand is usually near her ear.

TIMING -- "I think your timing is everything. If you don't have timing, if you do not feel comfortable, then you can't be consistent. Obviously, if you can't be consistent, you can't get the results you want." Yeagley says her timing begins with the push away of her ball and her first step. "I sometimes drop the ball too soon, and then try to hurry and catch up with my feet, and find myself at the line not able to stay down with the shot. So, for me, if I'm not comfortable, I check my push away first and go from there."

MENTAL GAME -- "I focus on one good shot at a time. I work at it one frame at a time," is what Yeagley says about dealing with poor shots, strike strings and distractions. "If I throw a couple of taps I double check myself, look at the people I am bowling with to see if they are pushing oil around causing carry down, think it through and try to get the ball to come into the pocket a little stronger. Usually I move back on the approach to try to get the ball to roll a little sooner on the lane, and if that doesn't work I move a board or two to the right."

Does she ever get nervous? "Oh, yes, I still get nervous." How does she handle it? "I tell myself to focus on one frame at a time. I can't do anything about the frames that have happened, and I can't do anything about the frames that haven't happened, so I focus on now."

What about the highs and lows in bowling? "It is the mental game. Are you concentrating? Are you loose? Are you thinking about other things? Are you focusing on one frame at a time? If the lanes do not drastically change, but your game has changed, then you have to go back to square one and try to do what you did when you were bowling well."

Trouble Spot: Staying relaxed and focused is key to good bowling. Bowlers and athletes in other sports say that when focus, relaxation and good results combine that is "being in the zone." Focusing on yourself and what you can do, rather than focusing on your surroundings and what you can't do, might help you relax.

Fast Facts

George Billick, Old Forge, Pa., registered his first 300 game in 1947 and second in 1951 on his way to 17 perfect games. Throughout his career, that also included more than a hundred 700 series, he missed the 300 only twice after shooting 11 strikes in a row. Using only a straight ball, his highest season average was a 223. He won the tournament of champions in 1956. He was inducted into the USBC Hall of Fame in 1982.

Mike Allan

MIKE ALLAN, 40, has six sanctioned 300 games, including back-to-back perfect games in 2005 when he hit a 300 in his last game in a Tuesday night league at Lane Glo Lanes North in Port Richey, Fla., and another 300 in his first game in a Thursday night league at Lane Glo Lanes South in New Port Richey.

Allan also has three 299s, and has averaged more than 200 in the past eight years, including a 215 in 2005-2006, a 210 in 2004-2005, and a 212 in 2003-2004. Born in Providence, R.I., Allan began bowling at the age of 9. A self-taught bowler who lives in Port Richey, he studies bowling books and magazines, watches the pros and says a key to success is "having a desire to win." He bowls in four leagues and competes in a number of tournaments.

Getting Better/Learning -- "If you want to be a better bowler," Allan says, "you have to have a clear mind, want to learn and be open to change. Watch the better bowlers. Bowl with them and against them when you can. Try to see what they do that you don't do. Strive to learn why you do not do well. And ask yourself, what can I do to be as good or better than the other guy?"

Follow Through -- "Follow through is a must. If you don't have follow through, you are going to throw bowling balls with nothing on them," Allan says. He tells bowlers to stay under the ball and get the ball out on the lane at least a foot beyond the foul line, reach to the target and follow through so your bowling hand nearly hits your head. For added action on the ball and additional hook when he needs it, Allan says he squeezes the ball after it leaves his thumb. "I like to get a lot of finger lift," he says.

Delivery -- "Of course you have to be smooth," Allan says, " but a

> **MIKE ALLAN**
> •Port Richey, Fla.
> •Back-to-back 300s at different centers.
> •Averages 210+ in past eight years.

lot of bowlers have the most difficulty in three main areas: staying balanced at the line, keeping the elbow in close to the body, and keeping the shoulders square to the target." He says bowlers should check their position after they release the ball. If the shoulders are not facing directly at the target -

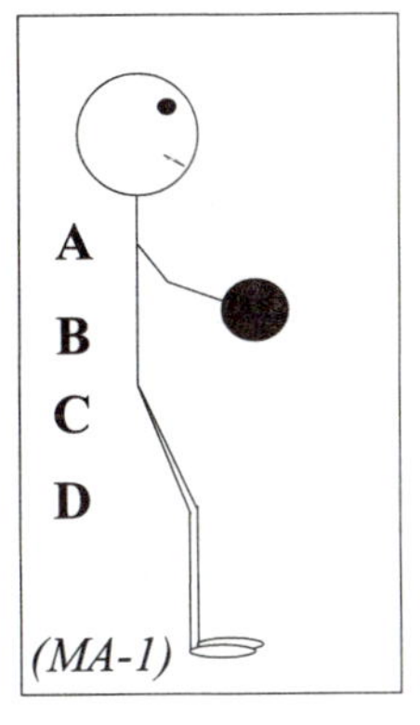

(MA-1)

- the pocket on strikes and the particular pins on spares -- they are going to miss or they are making some sort of adjustment to compensate for the poor body position. If bowlers are leaning sideways one way or the other or find they have to take some extra steps to stay balanced and square to the target after releasing the ball they need to work on better balance. "Keeping your shoulders level throughout the approach," Allan says,

STARTING (ADDRESS) POSITION: A - Back is straight. B - No forward lean. C - Position similar to sitting down. D - Knees bent slightly.

"and keeping down by bending slightly at the knees and waist without leaning forward should help you keep balanced." Allen recommends that bowlers bend at the knees as if they were about to sit down before starting the approach. (Fig. MA-1) "Of course," he says "not everyone can bend to the same degree, but if you can get down that will give you better balance and more lift on the ball."

Allan also blames "the elbow" for a lot of problems. "Check it out." he says. "When you see a bowler pull the ball past the head pin, or miss a spare to the left for a right handed bowler and to the right for a left handed bowler, you often see that bowler's elbow sticking out. Keep the elbow in and you will have much better control of the ball."

Trouble Spots: A number of older bowlers, especially those with bad knees, have trouble bending their sliding leg knee or bending both knees at the start and during the approach. A key in bowling is staying down and behind the ball. But if your knees will not cooperate, the next best thing is to strive for consistancy and balance. Whatever your shot -- as long as you are not lofting the ball and damaging the lanes -- being consistant with it will help you get better scores.

Aiming/Target -- Allan is a board bowler. "I try to get an idea of how my ball is working on the lanes, and use the boards for my target. I use the dots to line up my feet, and shoot at arrows for strikes and spares. I adjust my target throughout the game, but I adjust only when I know I have thrown a good ball and the lanes are changing," Allan says.

Trouble Spots: Of all the elements in bowling none is as important as knowing how to aim the bowling ball. If a bowler can not consistently hit a target, delivery and style become secondary. While there are many ways to aim for the pins, and those ways vary according to lane conditions, there are basically four methods of aiming: 1. Aiming at the pins. 2. Shooting at a dot, arrow or mark on the lane. 3. Shooting along an imaginary line on the lane from one mark to another. 4. Shooting to an area on the lane. Consistency in the entire approach, and balance in delivery are major factors in being able to hit a target.

(Fig. MA-2) LANE MARKINGS: Bowling lanes have a variety of markings to help bowlers find a target to better hit the pins. Various colored boards, not shown, are also used.

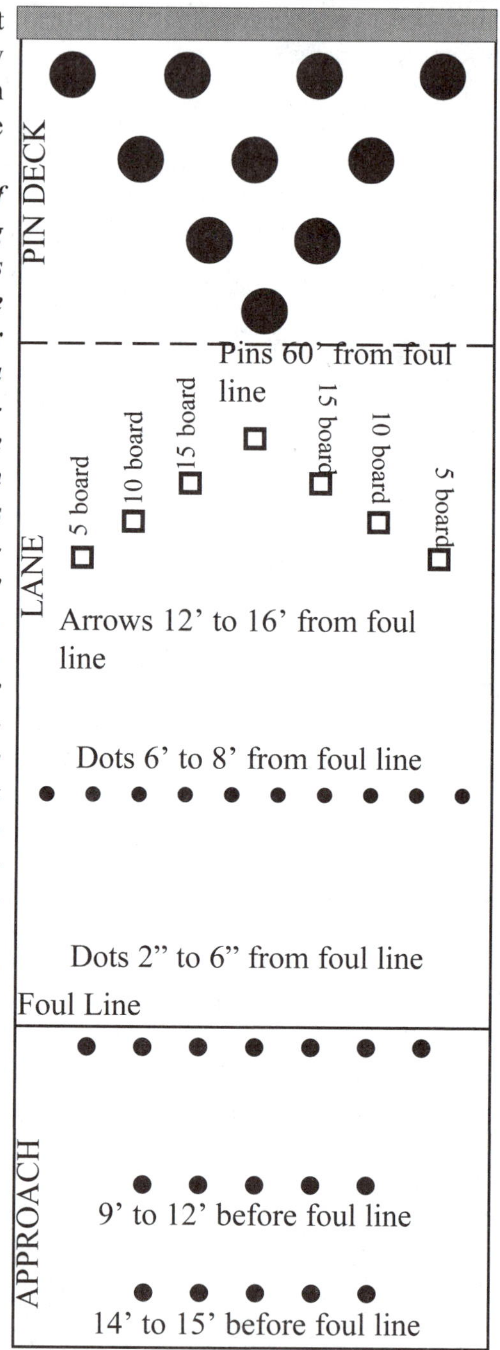

DEAN WOLF

DEAN WOLF, 42-year-old chiropractor from Reading, Pa., has manipulated the pins to such a degree that he is steadily closing in on bowling's most coveted record -- career 300 games.

In March 2006 Wolf rolled his 75th perfect game, moving him into a tie for second on the all-time list with Michigan's Joe Jimenez and just eight behind bowling's most prolific perfect-game shooter, professional Jeff Carter of Springfield, Ill.

Wolf has not thrown clusters of 300s, but in each year for the past 25 years has recorded two to four perfect games while averaging in the high 230s and posting 46 three-game 800 totals, including an 898 that ranks with one of the most odd big-series totals ever.

Wolf had eight strikes in a row in the first game that night in February 2005 at Bowlorama Lanes in Reading when the ball return refused to work. Lane management wanted to move the bowlers to another set of lanes, but Wolf and his teammates pleaded to finish the game on the same pair. Management gave in and for the last two frames returned each ball by hand. "That was great," Wolf said

DEAN WOLF

- **Reading, Pa.**
- **75 Perfect Games - second all-time.**
- **230+ Average 10 Consecutive Years.**
- **46 800s.**

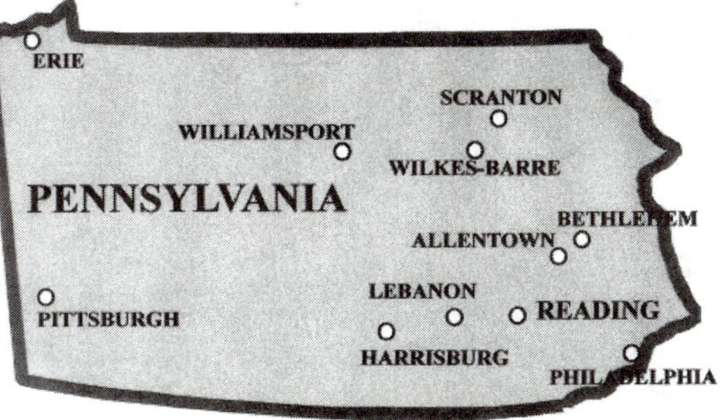

"but it also drew more attention on me so for the last four shots the lanes were quieter and it seemed like everyone was watching me. That was tough." Wolf struck through the 12th when he left a seven pin for a 299. Both teams moved to a working set of lanes for the second game, and Wolf rolled his 73rd 300 game. "At the time I thought it was a bad break, but the lanes were fresh with no carry-down oil because we did not get practice balls. I hit the first strike so I had a pretty good idea of what line to throw." Wolf continued striking through that game and the first 11 shots of the third game when his pocket hit on the 12th ball carried everything but an unyielding eight pin.

Wolf was born in Reading and began bowling at age 12. His first 200 game was a 211 when he was in the eighth grade. "My first game was a 42, so I'm no natural talent," he said. He was a member of the Professional Bowler's Aassociation (PBA) from 1983 through 1996. He quit professional bowling to concentrate on his chiropractic practice. "I just couldn't get away from my business that much."

Some of his other bowling honors include 15 singles championships in Pennsylvania's prestigious Dutchman Bolony Bowling Tournament, four Pennsylvania singles championships, the 1998 singles championship of the world's largest amateur tournament, the Hoinke Classic in Cincinnati, Ohio, and anchor of the 1992 American Bowling Congress Na-

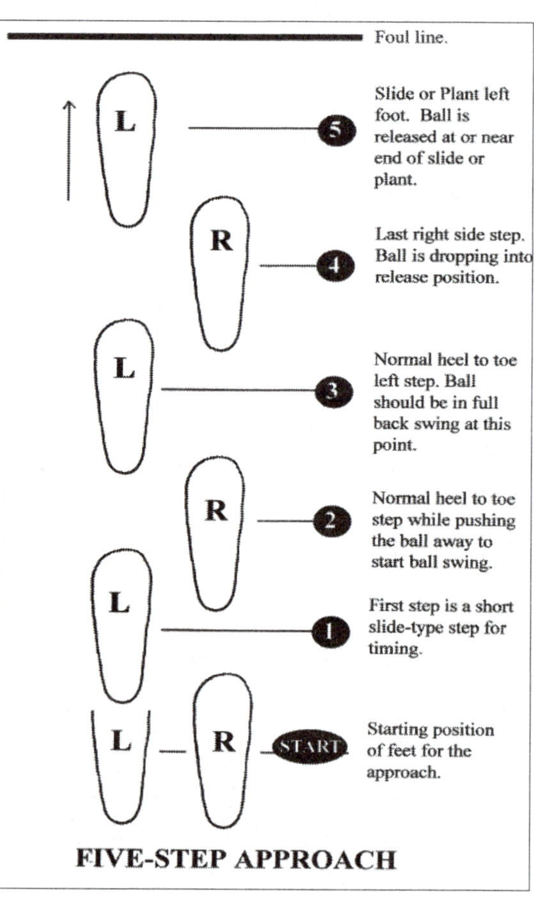

FIVE-STEP APPROACH

tional Tournament championship team. Wolf also has rolled fourteen 299 games and six 298 games and has not been under a 230 average in the past 10 years.

Mental Game -- Wolf says "don't try to think of too many things when you are on the approach. Concentrate on just doing one or two things perfectly."

Approach -- "I like the five-step approach," Wolf says, "with the first step, left foot, actually being my timing step. I take that step slowly, and then begin the ball push-away on the second, right foot, step." Wolf begins his approach with the ball about belt high. He naturally drops the ball on his push-away into a natural back swing that brings the ball up to his shoulder. "I don't think about the back swing at all. I think it is overrated. The back swing should be natural, and contingent on your body structure. In Reading there is an excellent bowler who is about 6 feet 5 inches tall whose back swing only reaches midway up his back, yet he is one of the best. His back swing is short because he is limited by ligamentous tone (tight muscles). And I know that because as a chiropractor I have worked on him." Wolf says his approach speed is "moderate," and he walks toward his target rather than trying to walk straight to the foul line. Wolf's final step ends with a short slide on the left foot. *(Note: See the five-step approach illustration on previous page.)*

Aim -- Wolf is a spot bowler. "I like to pick a target about 40 feet down the lane," he says, "but I recommend that less experienced bowlers concentrate on using the arrows for a target. It is easier to hit something closer to you, and hitting the target is a psychological boost." The right-hander's favorite line is to roll the ball across the 17-18 board at the arrows 15 feet out down to the 4, 5 or 6 board with a 15-board hook into the pocket. He sets up with his left foot on the 39 board. "That's my favorite line, but lane conditions dictate the best line. I most always adjust my target left, usually moving my feet two boards and my ball target one board each adjustment."

Loft -- In the case of ball loft what Wolf does and what he recommends are two different things. "I don't get the ball out far on the lanes. I sit it down quietly around the foul line. Sometimes that's not good because the ball rolls out (looses left-to-right rotation) too early so the finish is weak. Wolf can get away with that style because his ball rotation is exceptionally strong. "I recommend that bowlers attempt to get the ball out farther, at least a foot or two past the foul line to avoid rolling out."

Timing -- "Most of the problems in bowling have to do with timing. And timing starts on the approach. "If you want to develop and maintain good timing, you have to throw games. There is no substitute for practice," Wolf says. "I find to keep good timing I have to bowl often, not a lot, but often. When I'm getting ready for a tournament I bowl 15 minutes a day just trying to work on timing and feel." During his timing sessions Wolf bowls without pins. "The pins are just another thing to think about. Who cares if you threw a strike or the ball hooked early or whatever. When you work on timing the best thing to do is shadow bowl and bowl often."

Release -- Wolf uses three release positions, each conditional on lane conditions. "My strong position is with my thumb at 1 o'clock, with my mid position at noon and my weak position at 11 o'clock. In each I finish the release with my thumb at 10 o'clock. The constant in my release is a firm wrist. You have to have that to be consistent and get rotation on the ball." Wolf has practiced so much at maintaining a firm, flat wrist that he says he does not think about it. "I just throw that way."

Follow Through -- "The follow through has to be there to get big scores. That doesn't mean your hand has to go to the ceiling on the follow through or even to 45 degrees. The position of the follow through is different for everyone. A good follow through means you have to come through the ball with a firm wrist to get ball rotation, to get power."

Power Bowling -- Although Wolf throws a very strong ball he does not consider himself a power bowler -- a cranker. Crankers are those bowlers (Pete Weber was an example on the professional level before he lessened his back swing and ball speed) who throw a fast ball with exceptional revolutions from a back swing that brings the ball high over the bowlers head. "They are fun to watch," he says. "I think anyone who can do that should do it. Later, if you want to ease off you can. But if you don't learn that style at a young age, it is nearly impossible to develop later."

Stringing Strikes -- "It probably will sound trite, but my approach is to play one ball at a time. I try to throw the best shot I can every time, and if I am lucky I throw eight or nine perfect shots a night. How does he handle his nerves? "Don't let anybody tell you they don't get nervous when they're approaching a 300 game or some other big score. I have seen pros get so nervous they shake, and then get up and throw a strike. I try to forget the nerves, work on one shot at a time and concentrate on throwing a perfect ball." Wolf said dealing with nerves gets easier with more success. "I'm usually a little more nervous in the early part of a bowling season than I am in December or later."

Spares -- Wolf throws a thumb-first straight ball for spares. His spare ball is a very old 16-pound Brunswick Mineralite. "It has only a four-diget serial number." For strikes he throws a 16-pound ball with a relaxed finger-tip grip. *(NOTE: Brunswick introduced the Mineralite ball in 1906. It was made mostly of rubber, was the first mass-production ball, and replaced the wooden balls of the time.)*

Practice -- Wolf bowls in two leagues a week and 10 to 12 tournaments a season. "I practiced a lot more when I was learning to bowl than I do now. He has a practice lane in the basement of his house, but says generally league and tournament bowling keeps him sharp. "When I practice I work on a single shot and try to see how many times I can throw the same shot." He does not bowl in summer leagues, preferring to rest and come into the bowling season fresh. "In May I start getting tired of bowling, but by August I'm anxious to get going again."

Learning -- Wolf does not believe there is such a thing as a natural bowler. "You only get good by practicing," he says. "Try to bowl with the best bowlers. Watch them. Learn from them." He also advocates learning from reading about bowling and watching the PBA events on television. He watches the PBA classic events on ESPN.

Fast Facts

Dick Weber, Dec. 23, 1929, was PBA Bowler of the Year in 1961, 1963, 1965. He won 26 regular PBA titles, five senior PBA championships and four National All-Stars over five decades. In 1991, at the age of 62, Weber suffered a mild stroke at a senior PBA tournament in Lady Lake, Fla. He was hospitalized for a week in Leesburg. Eight months later he bowled in the opening senior tournament of the 1992 season at the Showboat Hotel's 106-lane center in Las Vegas. Weber first won PBA championships in 1959 in Paramus, N.J., and Dayton, Ohio. Weber died in St. Louis Feb. 13, 2003, at the age of 75.

Karen Rosenburg

KAREN ROSENBURG,

Rolla, Mo., was tired that night Dec. 12, 2001, when she bowled an 878, the highest sanctioned three-game total in women's bowling history.

"We had been moving all day at the office, so when I went to bowl I was pretty tired. But as it turned out that helped me keep my feet slow during the approach, which is a key for me. After that, everything went right." Rosenburg, 37 years old at the time, threw games of 299, 279 and 300 in the Coachlite Queens League at Coachlite Lanes in Rolla to break the then four-year-old record of 877 set by Jackie Mitskavich of Van Wert, Ohio.

Was she nervous? "Yeah. How could I not be. But was I thinking about an 878 and the record? No. I had no clue whatsoever," she said. "I had 299 on my first game. My teammates had not seen a 300, so I really wanted one for them." She left a 10 pin on the last shot of that game off a strong pocket hit. She finished her 279 second game with nine consecutive strikes after a 10-pin leave and a spare in the third frame. "I never dreamed I would shoot a 300 in the last game, but then after I hit the first eight I thought 'wow, I could shoot a 300 here, and I don't want to let my team down again.'" She did not know she had a chance at the record until after she had broken it. "I had an 847 in the

> **KAREN ROSENBURG**
>
> **Rolla, Mo.**
> **Highest All-Time**
> **Series: 878.**
> **Six 300s.**
> **210+ Average past**
> **18 years.**

Missouri State Tournament 11 days earlier," she said, "and I was just trying for another 800."

Rosenburg, a right-handed bowler, hit the 1-3 pocket on all 36 strike attempts, and during her second and third games strung 21 strikes. Onlookers say her ball speed varied less than a half-mile per hour and was about 15 miles per hour the entire night.

While the record was extra special, bowling big scores and seeing big scores was nothing new for Rosenburg. She grew up in Cape Girardeau, Mo., in a bowling family -- "everybody in the family bowled" -- and met her husband, professional bowler David Rosenburg, in the Cape Girardeau bowling center. "He came to the Cape for a bowling tournament, and I happened to be there bowling. After the tournament David and a mutual friend asked me to join them for something to eat, I said no, and the rest is history."

In 1994 she won a regional Lady's Professional Bowling Tournament and David won a regional Professional Bowling Association championship a weekend apart. David, part-time operator of a pro bowling shop in Rolla, bowled on the PBA tour from 1986 through 1988. He has recorded 33 perfect games, 16 three-game 800s and seven regional PBA championships. Karen has six 300s, four 800s, three 299s, one 298, two 296s (left the bucket on each), and has won three Missouri singles championships, three all-events titles, was on a state championship women's team, and was a member with David and another couple in winning the Missouri mixed team championships in 1991 and 2001. Karen began bowling at age 8, was in a junior league at age 13, and has averaged 210 or higher for the past 18 years, with a high of 226 in 2003.

The Rosenburgs have a 15-year-old son and a seven-month old daughter. When they are not working or bowling they go camping, snow skiing, horseback riding and fishing.

Approach -- Rosenburg uses a five-step approach. She concentrates on walking slowly and keeping her elbow in. She begins with the ball chest high. She pushes the ball out on her second step, letting it drop into her back swing. She walks straight to the foul line, rather than veering to the target.

Target -- "I look at the first row of dots, then down the lane to where I want the ball to go," Rosenburg says. "I drawn an imaginary line down the lane to the break point, and throw my ball down that line." Rosenburg says she does not put a lot of turn on her ball, so accuracy is the big part of her game. Her favorite shot is a "down and in" ball between the five and eight boards. Occasionally she shoots off the 15 board.

Timing -- "Timing is everything for everybody. For me it is keeping my feet slow, keeping my elbow in and staying down at the line," Rosenburg said. "It is also getting to the line balanced, getting through the ball without jerking up, and staying down and getting through the ball to get pin reaction and good carry." Rosenburg agrees that timing is difficult to maintain and even harder to correct. "You have to tell yourself to do the things that work for you," she says, "if something isn't working you have to try to change something because the same thing does not work every night." Rosenburg says she gets a lot of help from her husband. "David knows my game best, and he can tell me exactly what I'm doing wrong when I'm off. If you can get somebody who knows your game -- a teammate, friend or spouse -- to help you, that's a big plus."

Back Swing -- "I don't think much about the back swing. I think mine is about normal for what normal people have. I try to be smooth."

Loft -- Rosenburg does not loft her ball in setting it down four to six inches past the foul line. "I try to keep the ball low."

Release -- Rosenburg cups the ball in her approach and stays behind and under it when she releases it with a firm wrist and a thumb rotation from around 11 o'clock to 10 o'clock. "I try to get a good roll on the ball," she says, "and when I do the last thing I feel is the ball on my finger tips." She throws a 15-pound ball with a fingertip grip.

Follow Through -- "You definitely need it." Rosenburg says her hand follows through to her target and finishes over her head. "You have to have follow through to get the ball rolling and to hit the target."

Mental Game -- "For me the mental game is "thinking about what I need to do." She says she repeats to herself in her approach routine the part of the game she needs to emphasize -- keeping her feet slow, keeping her ball speed up, keeping her eye on the target, staying down and keeping her elbow in.

Stringing Strikes -- "I don't think about the three or four in a row. I think one frame and one ball at a time."

Spares -- Rosenburg does not carry a special spare ball. "I just use my weakest hooking ball," she says. She throws a flattened straight ball from the left and right corners for the 10 and 7 pins, and throws a small hook for all other spares.

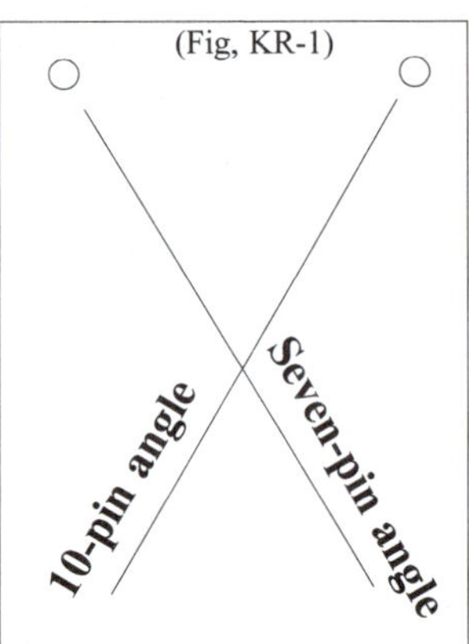

10-PIN & 7-PIN SPARES: Recommended ball path for covering the seven pin and 10 pin is to use as much of the lane as possible. The ball for both spares will roll near the center arrow.

Ed Duer

ED DUER believes bowling is best when it is kept reasonably simple. In keeping it simple since he started bowling in 1966 at age 32 he has registered 51 sanctioned perfect games in 12 different bowling centers. Thirty three of the 300 games -- including 11 in 1995 -- were registered since the 71-year-old New Port Richey, Fla., retiree turned 60.

"When I was learning to bowl I just tried to make it as simple as possible. I keep my wrist movement to a minimum, I keep my arm straight, I roll the ball from one spot to another in a line to the pocket, and when I get the line right I try to keep throwing it there," Duer says.

Duer really got the bowling bug in 1967, his second year of league bowling. "I went to Miami to bowl with my team in ABC National Tournament," he says. "In the convention center they had guys standing in the back putting up big Xs when anybody got a strike. I was just a 156 average bowler, and I was just there to bowl with my team. I didn't enter any of the other events. I had the first seven strikes in a row, was shaking in my shoes, and ended up with a 240 something, but it was such a damn thrill to me I decided it was a lot of fun and I was going to keep doing it. The excitement of watching a guy put those big Xs up there on the wall by my name was quite a thrill."

Since that time the Wildwood, N.J., native who only began league bowling when he moved to Florida, has had

> **ED DUER**
>
> **71 Years Old.**
> **51 Perfect Games,**
> **33 Since Age 60.**
> **Twenty-two 800s.**
> **Twenty years with**
> **200+ average.**

many bowling thrills. He has recorded twenty-two 800s, has won two Senior Bowling Association championships, won four National Senior Bowler's Tournament championsips against some of the biggest names in the professional ranks, has won four Super Senior Tournaments in Orlando, Fla, for bowlers older than 60, three West Coast senior tournaments, and has competed in 34 United States Bowling Congress (formerly ABC) national bowling tournaments since 1976. He has averaged more than 200 for 20 years, including a 230 in 2004-2005 at Hudson Bowl in Hudson, Fla. In 2002 he was inducted into the Suncoast (Clearwater-Pasco County, Fla.) Bowling Association Hall of Fame.

In 1981 Duer rolled a very unusual, unsanctioned but bonafide 300 game when he strung 12 real strikes while bowling across six lanes in a no-tap tournament at the now-defunct Richey Lanes in New Port Richey.

One of his greatest successes? "That was winning a local tournament with my grandson," Duer said. "He told everyone 'I'm going to win this tournament because my grandpa is going to bowl with me,' and we did."

Approach -- Duer is a right handed bowler who uses a four-step approach. He begins his approach by stepping with his right foot, while pushing his ball forward at the same time. "The push-away sets up my timing," he says. He usually holds his ball about waist high, but when he wants more ball speed he holds it higher. Most of the time he walks straight to his target. "If I have to throw the ball right, then I walk on an angle to my target." His approach speed is fairly fast.

Back Swing -- Duer's back swing is a key component in his striking power and ability to hit the 1-3 pocket consistently. "I control the path of the ball by speed," he says. "If the lanes are dry (hooking more) I put more speed on the ball, and if the lanes are oily I throw a slower ball with less back swing." Duer does not force the

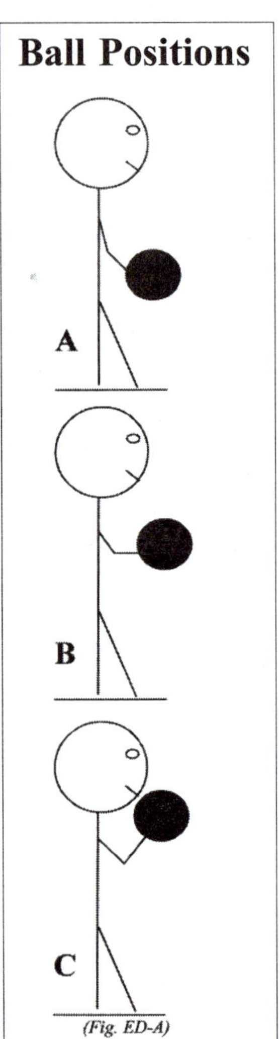

A. Starting ball position for minimum back swing and ball speed.
B. Starting ball position for medium back swing and ball speed.
C. Starting ball position for high back swing and faster ball speed.

back swing or his speed. "The back swing is controlled by where I hold the ball when I start my approach. I hold the ball higher in front of me to get more back swing, and lower the ball to reduce the back swing. From the starting position I just push the ball away from me and let gravity take its course." (Fig. ED-A)

Target -- Duer is a line bowler. (Fig. ED1) He uses three check points to hit the pocket. "I try to make sure my arm crosses my target, usually a dot at the foul line, and my ball rolls over a targeted dot on the second set of dots and follows a line across a target at the diamonds arrows," he says. "When I get the ball lined up so it hits the pocket, I just keep throwing there. Of course, when the oil pattern changes I have to move left."

Loft -- Duer's ball consistently hits the lanes just past the first row of dots past the foul line. Does he adjust his loft to compensate for lane conditions? "No. You know I have heard a lot of people say if the heads are real dry you have to get the ball past the heads. I have never had that problem. I

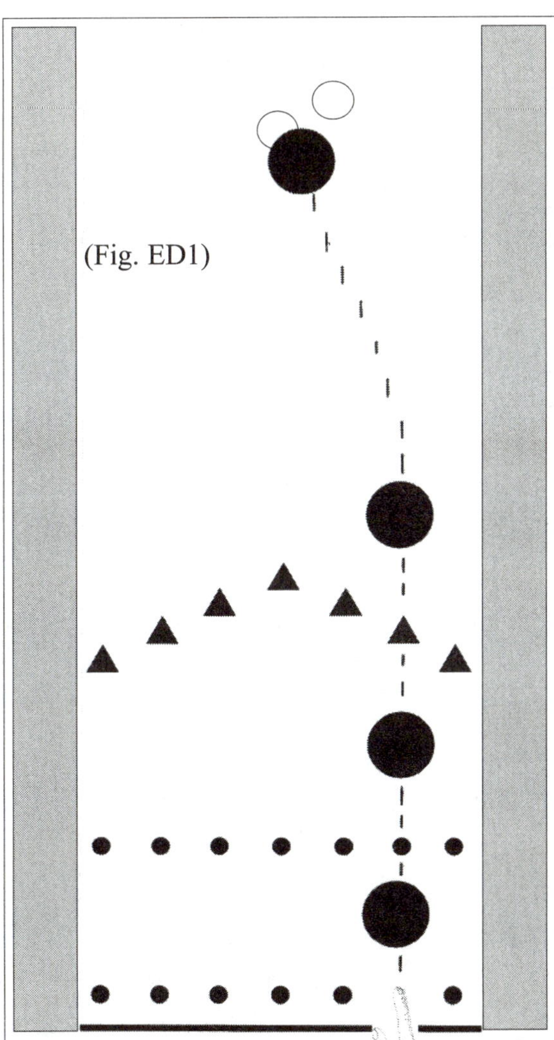

LINE BOWLING: In line bowling the bowler tries to roll the ball from one point to another on an imaginary line that will enter the pocket.

could always throw the ball hard enough to get through the heads."

Ball Release -- "I hold the ball in the palm of my hand with my thumb facing between 11 and 12 o'clock. When I release the ball my thumb is usually at about 11 o'clock, my wrist is always firm, and I feel the ball go off my fingers," Duer explained. He says an indication that he is throwing the ball correctly comes when "my fingers tingle." In his basic release he keeps his hand under the ball, but on occasion he says he does throw a "suitcase" (hand on top of the ball with fingers on the side) when lanes are especially oily.

Ball Rotation -- Duer's ball rolls in the direction of the pins rather than on a side-to-side rotation. It is classified as a forward roll. "If you get good rotation on the ball it hits harder and carries better." Duer gets strong rotation by getting his thumb out of it and rolling it with his fingers.

Follow Through -- "I try to make sure I lift the ball at the end, and I follow through enough to stick my thumb in my eye," Duer says. "If you just stop your hand motion when you release the ball, it just plunks out on the lane and will not do anything. I try to make sure I hit (lift) the ball at the end."

Stringing Strikes -- "I still get a little nervous when I have eight or nine in a row. I try to say I don't, but I do," Duer says. "At that point, though, I try to think about something besides bowling, something good, a good meal or going sailing or riding a motorcycle when I'm waiting. When I get up to bowl, I just concentrate on hitting the mark."

Timing -- "Basically, bowling is all timing. If your timing is right, then you can bowl all right," Duer says. He says his timing is mainly dependent on pushing his ball out at the same time he starts his four-step approach on his right foot. "If I get to the line with my shoulders square, I am in time."

Mental Game -- "My mental approach is to think I can knock all the pins down all the time. You gotta believe you can do that or you might as well not go down there," Duer says. "Don't get mad if you miss a 10 pin or seven pin or whatever, that just ruins your game. Nobody is perfect, so once in a while you miss them. It is not a life and death thing to me. It is just bowling. So if I miss, I miss. I just didn't throw the ball well." Duer says.

Spares -- Duer seldom misses a spare. "I don't look at the pins. I just know what spot I want to throw the ball over to hit a particular pin." He does not change balls for spares.

Ball --Duer uses a 16-pound ball with a relaxed fingertip grip. "I like a ball with a leverage weight."

Practice -- Duer bowls in five leagues and a number of tournaments throughout the year so he does not often schedule a practice session. During warm-up practice for league competition he has a routine he follows that includes a first ball just to get loose, a second ball down the eight board to check oil conditions. "If I throw the ball up the eight board and it doesn't get to the pocket, that means they have oiled a little further out, and I have to move right a little," he says. "Now days they make the lanes dry outside, so you have to move right to hit the pocket so I move over two boards and throw the ball down the six board. Sometimes I have to go to the three or four board." Duer says if he has time he also throws down the 10 or 11 board to check the oil pattern to see how much his ball moves to the left, and he throws over the five board to see if the ball will jump left. In both cases he is checking to see if the ball "hangs" in the oil or jumps left because the lanes are dry. That not only helps him find the pocket, but also helps in spare situations. "You have to know if the ball will move left or hang," he says.

Fast Facts

Where are the most bowlers?

According to the United States Bowling Congress, Michigan is the perennial leader. In the 2004-2005 season some 262,536 men, women and youth joined the USBC in that state. Ohio ranked second with 204,380 members. California was third with 170,106 members. New Hampshire had the least number of bowlers with just 4,320.

Detroit is the leading bowling city in the U.S. with 97,047 sanctioned players.

There were 51,162 sanctioned 300 games in the 2004-2005 season, according to the USBC. Of that total, 1,060 were shot by women. There also were 15,903 three-game 800s, of which 207 were hit by women. On a down note of sorts, 21,401 bowlers missed perfect games on their last ball as there were that many 299s.

Bob Blechner

BOB BLECHNER, 64-year-old semiretired New York City bank officer, insurance broker and tax consultant, bowled just once a week until 1994 when he moved to Florida and found more time for the sport.

In the past four years he has averaged more than 200 with a 222 season in 2003 and a 217 in 2004 that included a sanctioned 300 game. Today the Bayonet Point, Fla., resident has one of the smoothest, easy-on-the-body bowling styles a bowler could have. He believes that success in bowling comes from consistency, and "consistency is much easier to achieve if bowling is made as simple as possible without sacrificing ball impact."

Approach -- "I use short steps because it helps me keep better balance, which of course translates into making it easier to be accurate and more consistent."

Trouble Spot: Many bowlers approach the shot and foul line at varying speeds. Sometimes the approach speed is dependent on the shot the bowler is trying to make, and sometimes approach speed changes for no apparent reason. Approach speed is a major part of timing the release of the ball in coordination with the bowler's slid or foot plant and arm swing.

BOB BLECHNER

Bayonet Point, Fla.
64 Years Old
One Perfect Game
Averages 217+

Release -- Blechner throws from behind and under the ball with his thumb at about noon to 11 and rotates his thumb counterclockwise to about 10 when he releases the ball. He keeps his wrist and fingers firm. "I like to get solid fingers into the ball on every shot, and increase the rotation by spreading my index and little fingers wide on the ball, and decreasing the rotation and hook by bringing my index and little fingers closer to the middle fingers. You have to have a ball that has authority, one that comes into the pins with a pow," he says.

Follow Through -- Blechner's follow through is consistent. "I get the ball out on the lane about a foot and come through the ball with my hand in one continual motion. I kind of touch my head, and that tells me my follow through is there." As most high scoring bowlers, Blechner says "I've never seen a really good bowler without a good follow through."

Adjusting -- "I consistently stand on the 22 board and shoot over the 10 board. Because I keep my approach, release and ball speed as close to the same as possible every time, I usually adjust just a few boards left or right on my starting position to meet lane conditions," Blechner said. If the lanes are extra dry or extra oily he may move as much as three or four boards left or right. His ball speed is 20+ mph.

Trouble Spot: Figuring out changing lane conditions (see lane conditions on Pages 55-58) is a major part of bowling. There are a number of systems for changing, but far too often bowlers make drastic changes without giving the small changes a chance first. Basically, a right-handed bowler should move the starting position to the right to get the ball further left, and to the left to get the ball further to the right.

Spares -- Blechner, unlike most of today's top bowlers, uses just one ball most of the time, and uses the same ball for strikes and spares. "I shoot all the spares except the 10-pin exactly as I throw the strike ball. For the 10 pin I line up with the left gutter and walk toward the 10-pin hitting the 20-board or fourth arrow with a little more speed and little less fingers in the ball. I always use as much of the lane as possible, shooting far cross-lane on the seven, and square my shoulders to whatever my target is."

Fast Facts

Marion Ladewig, Grand Rapids. Mich., dominated the female side of bowling in the 1950s and 1960s. She won the U.S. Open eight times, taking the first five. She won the World Invitational five times, and was named bowler of the year nine times between 1950 and 1963. Inducted into the WIBC Hall of Fame in 1983, she began bowling as a teenager and continued to bowl into her 80s. She was born Oct. 30, 1914.

•**Patty Costello**, Scranton, Pa., won the Maryland State Junior Girls championship as a 15-year-old, and turned pro at the age of 21. She won three consecutive pro tournaments in 1972 and 1976. She was named a *Bowlers Journal* All-American eight times.

Jeff K. Campbell II

JEFF K. CAMPBELL II,

New Castle, Pa., defied the odds that magical night June 12, 2004, in New Castle's Colonial Lanes when he became only the sixth bowler in bowling's 109-year history to register a perfect three-game 900 series.

"The 900 felt unreal, unbelievably unreal," Campbell said nearly two years after his remarkable night. "It was one of those things you kind of dream about, but for it to really happen was unexplainable. It was so exciting. It was something I will never forget. I really can't describe it too well."

Campbell, only 22 at the time but imbued with a veteran's experience after eight year's of youth tournament competition and hours and hours of training from his bowling father, said nervousness only became a factor in the 10th frame of the third game. "When I got the first one in the 10th (his 34th consecutive strike) I started getting a little nervous. When I got the second one (his 35th) I really wasn't quite as nervous as I thought I would be. I always thought 'man, if I ever got that many in a row I don't know what I will do.' My thought then was 'I will probably never ever be here again, I will probably never have a chance at this again, so make it count.'"

> # JEFF K. CAMPBELL II
>
> - New Castle, Pa.
> - 24 Years Old
> - 900 Series was 6th in bowling history.

Campbell's last shot, the 36th strike, was a pocket strike, as were all but three or four of all the strikes. Throughout the night Campbell did not throw a crossover or even a hard nose hit. "There were a couple of light, shaker hits," he said, "and one where I had a 10-pin standing and a slow roller came across the deck and took it out."

He was averaging in the 230s before that night, so it was not unusual that most of his shots were in the pocket. "It just got to the point after catching a couple of breaks that I thought 'wow, I don't know if I'm ever going to miss again.'"

The first ever 900 series was recorded Feb. 2, 1997, by Jeremy Sonnenfeld in Lincoln, Neb. Tony Raventini of Milwaukee hit the second one Nov. 9,1998, in Greenfield, Wisc. Vince Wood of Moreno Valley, Calif., hit it in 1999, Robby Portalatin of Jackson, Mich., rolled 36 strikes in a row in 2000, and James Hylton of Salem, Ore., posted a 900 in 2001. Darren Pomije, New Prague, Minn., hit the seventh sanctioned perfect triple Dec. 9, 2004. The last 900 series was recorded in April 22, 2006, by Mark Wukoman in Greenfield, Wisc.

According to mathematician Derek Eshelbrenner of Independence, Kans., a 900 series has occurred once in every 760 million three-game sets since Sonnenfeld's first one in 1997.* Figuring the statistics since the American Bowling Congress was founded in 1895 to the present is impossible because advances in equipment and technical skills have drastically changed the game.

Despite the odds, Campbell came close March 30, 2006, to duplicating his 900 fete. He set the Amarillo, Texas, City record with an 869 series on games of 279, 290 and 300. Only two 10 pins, one in the seventh frame of the first game and one in the first frame of the second game, is all that kept him from his second 900 series.

Campbell was named an NCBCA All-American at Vincennes University in Vincennes, Ind., in 2003 and 2004 when the college team under NJCAA Hall of Fame coach Gary Sparks won back-to-back national championships. "Coach Sparks is a great coach, and he helped me develop an all-around game." Campbell averaged 205 in two years at Vincennes. In

The Odds of a 900

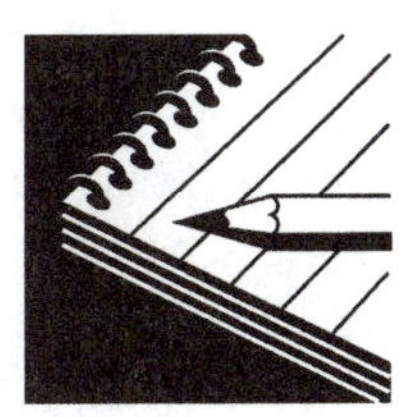

**Mathematician Derek Eshelbrenner's odds on the likelihood of bowling a 900 three-game series are based on five million bowlers participating in a 36-week league each year over 30 years. The figures do not take into consideration skill levels, but are based solely on numbers. He says if a 900 was simply a matter of luck, as in a drawing, the average person might get a 900 if he or she bowled a three-game series every hour of every day of every week for 87,000 years. If the same bowler hit the lanes only once a week to bowl a series, that bowler would stand a chance of a 900 if he or she bowled 14.4 million years. That same person would need nearly 29 million years to get two 900s.*

2004, his final year at Vincennes, he was BWAA Bowler of the Year runner-up.

Campbell now lives in Canyon, Tex., where he competes in three sanctioned leagues and holds averages ranging from 229 to 235. He practices nearly every day. He has seven career 800s, 11 300s, five 299s and one 298. In 2005, he and his fiance, Megan Larson of Canyon, Tex., won the Mixed Doubles championship in the *Bowler's Journal* Tournament.

LARSON

Approach --Campbell used a five-step approach. "I'm a shorter guy, 5 feet 5 inches tall, and the extra step gives me a little more ball speed and helps me with my timing," he says. "I used to use four steps, but was rushing, so I added a little push-away step with the left foot that allows me to push the ball away a little bit later, and get my tempo right so I don't arrive at the line ahead of the ball." Campbell begins his approach with his ball held at midsection level. His first step with the left foot is a little slide step. On his right foot step he pushes his ball out and up and allows it to drop, straightening his arm and flowing into his back-swing. He says his approach speed is moderate, and his ball speed is 16 to 17 miles per hour. He ends his approach with a short slide on his left foot, and releases his ball at the completion of the slide. Whether Campbell walks straight to the foul line or to his target depends on the how he is playing the lanes. "If I am playing the gutter, I get far right and walk straight toward my target. If I am playing further out with a little swing, I actually drift a little left in the approach and open up (face the target) at the end." Campbell drifts to the right on his approach when he plays a tighter, inside line to the pocket.

Target -- It used to be that accuracy was the thing -- splitting arrows or boards or half boards. But now, with today's technology, when bowlers can open the lane up and generate high revolutions on the ball, there are more feel bowlers. "If I have to focus on a board or target I'll do that, but when I am bowling my best I get a feel for an area. That gives me more room to hit the pocket." Campbell's favorite line is a down and in shot along the two or three board, especially on sport conditions, and shorter oil patterns.

Ball rotation -- Campbell says he achieves strong side-to-side rotation on the ball by getting his hand under the ball at his push-away and keeping it there on the back-swing and downswing until he brings the ball just past his sliding foot when he releases it with a thumb rotation from 3 o'clock to 10 o'clock. "I get additional help in the rotation by delaying the hit as long as possible and by getting the ball out on the lane low and long. I keep my fingers below the equator of the ball."

Timing -- "I can just tell if my timing is off. If I am a little fast with my feet, I try to get the ball started sooner. The biggest part of timing for me in my five-step approach is the second step when I push the ball away. That's where I work on timing, and that's where I can tell if it's on or off."

Back Swing -- "The back swing is pretty important in my style because it helps me generate the speed I need." Campbell brings the ball to just above his shoulder on his back swing, which all begins with his lifting motion in his push-away.

Loft -- Campbell does not loft the ball in terms of throwing the ball above his release point. He subscribes to bowling coach John Jowdy's recommendation to get the ball out low and long. Campbell releases his ball closer to the foul line when the lanes are oily and he wants more roll on the ball, and he gets the ball out farther when the lanes are dry. "When the lanes start breaking down, I get behind the ball a little more and get it out farther so the ball does not roll out too soon."

Release -- "My go-to game is to keep my wrist locked with my hand under the ball. I try to lead with the inside of my forearm to help me stay behind the ball. I like to have my thumb at about 3 o'clock and rotate it to around 10 o'clock at the release." Campbell says a strong wrist position is very important and "helps you do a lot of things with the ball."

Follow Through -- "Follow through is a key component of the game. If you find yourself getting lazy on a shot, basically your not following through, you are not finishing the shot," Campbell says. He says he reminds himself in his pre-shot routine to follow through. Rather than loft the ball, Campbell keeps it low while "getting out on the lane." "My hand finishes out toward the pins, not high, out."

Stringing Strikes -- Campbell says he tries to roll every ball as if it is the first frame. "When I'm stringing strikes I look at every frame as a new frame, focusing on the task at hand rather than what has happened."

Spares -- As with most top bowlers, Campbell throws straight at spares. "I use my weakest ball," he says, "and flatten it out." He uses 15 pound balls drilled with fingertip grips.

Adjusting -- "The more you bowl the more you understand how the lanes breakdown. You need to go into the center with some kind of game plan based on the oil pattern for those lanes. (Many centers post a diagram of the oil patterns they use.) Then, throughout the block, stick to your plan as long as it is working." He also says to watch other bowlers to see how the successful bowlers are playing the lanes. Campbell says he has no adjustment formula, but rather changes lines, balls and releases depending on lane conditions.

Pre-shot Routine -- "I think the pre-shot routine is a very important part of the game," Campbell says. "When I get up to bowl I go through a checklist making sure my feet are lined up with the target, my shoulders and hips are lined up with the target, and tell myself to swing through the target."

Mental Game -- "You have to screen out the highs and lows," Campbell says. "If you let yourself get too high, then all you are doing is setting yourself up to crash. You have to be able to maintain a certain focus. You also have to be able to shake off bad shots and taps, and tell yourself to grind it out, make your own breaks and get back in the game." Campbell says he does a lot of deep breathing to relax, does a lot of positive self talk, and establishes a regular pre-shot routine. "I wipe the ball the same amount of times every time, hit the rosin the same amount of times, and give myself the reminders I need." Campbell says he also reminds himself that no matter what shot he threw, he has to focus on the next shot using his saying "that's what, so what, now what?"

By the Numbers

ALL STRIKES: Twelve strikes in a row from the first frame through the 10th frame is a perfect 300 games.

11 STRIKES: If you throw 11 strikes in a row from the first through the 10th frame, your score will be 290 plus whatever you get on the twelfth ball. If you throw 11 strikes in a row from the second frame through the 10th frame, your score will be 270 plus whatever score you had in the first frame. The 11-strike game can range from a 270 (two gutter balls in the first frame) to a 290 (a spare in the first frame). The lowest possible score with 11 strikes in a game but not in a row is a 250. To hit that score the bowler must have a double gutter ball in any middle frame.

200 GAME: A bowler must have at least one strike during the 10 frames to hit a 200 game. The highest possible all-spare game score is 190.

HELP IN A NUTSHELL

This section is a "nutshell" view -- a compendium -- of the bowling tips and ideas offered by our better bowlers in the Bowling Lessons section of *Bowler's Handbook*.   Here, in a glance, you can read what the better bowlers say about the various aspects and elements of bowling. For more detailed information, however, go back to Bowling Lessons section to see the complete comments by each bowler.

LEARNING

How do you learn to bowl?

Do you go to the lanes with some friends, as most people do, and simply try it with varying degrees of success? Do you learn from parents and other relatives, as many, many bowlers have done? Most good bowlers would answer our leading question by saying "get coaching and start out correctly so you don't have to overcome the bad habits you will pickup when you try to teach yourself."

Our better bowlers seem to have several things in common in their learning stages. They spent a lot of time learning, they were not exceptionally successful at first, they got help and sought help from good bowlers and coaches, and they participated in bowling programs.

Here are the main points offered by our better bowlers on learning to bowl:

Baginski -- "When I was 16 and 17 years old and trying to really improve I bowled at least 100 games a week every week for a year and a half. The local lanes had a special of three hours for $5, and I took advantage of that."

Yeagley -- She started bowling at age six, participated in junior bowling programs, attended Pennsylvania State University's summer bowling programs, and credits the junior bowling program in her home town and her husband, William, with helping her learn hand positions and more advanced techniques.

Allan -- If you want to be a better bowler you have to have a clear mind, want to learn and be open to change. Watch the better bowlers.

Bowl with them and against them when you can. Try to see what they do that you don't do."

Wolf -- "You only get good by practicing. Try to bowl with the best bowlers. Watch them. Learn from them."

Rosenburg -- She was raised in a family of bowlers, and began bowling at the age of eight. She bowled a number of years in junior league competition.

Duer -- "When I was learning to bowl I just tried to make it as simple as possible. I keep my wrist movement to a minimum. I keep my arm straight, I roll the ball from one spot to another in a line to the pocket, and when I get the line right I try to keep throwing it there."

Campbell -- Campbell is a product of eight years of competition in Pennsylvania youth leagues and coaching from his father and Hall of Fame Coach Gary Sparks at Vincennes University in Vincennes, Ind.

APPROACH

The approach is the key to good timing in bowling. Whether using a five-step, four-step, or three-step approach, all of our top bowlers say the ball push-away is instrumental in starting the back swing, controlling ball speed and arriving at the line slightly ahead of the ball so the ball can be delivered with a sound release and follow through.

Speed of the approach is up to the individual bowler, as is length of steps, position of the ball in the starting setup and approach conclusion in a slide or plant. The constants in the approach recommended by our bowling experts are an early push away, natural back swing, a direct path to the target, good flow and consistency.

Here are the main points offered by our better bowlers on approach:

Baginski -- "The key is to put your ball in the same place all the time for the strike shots, and move your starting point -- where you place your feet -- to adjust to the lane. Remember, you don't want to play where you want to play, you want to play where the lane wants you to play."

Yeagley -- "I try to make sure I push the ball away on my first step, and I don't go too high on my back swing."

Wolf -- "I like the five-step approach, with the first step, left foot, actually being my timing step. I take that step slowly, and then begin the ball push-away on the second, right foot, step."

Duer -- "The push-away sets up my timing." He uses a four-step approach, pushing the ball away on his first step.

Blechner -- "I use short steps because it helps me keep better balance, which of course translates into making it easier to be accurate and more consistent."

Campbell -- He uses the five-step approach. "I'm a shorter guy, 5 feet 5inches tall, and the extra step gives me a little more ball speed and helps me with my timing."

TIMING

Timing often is that elusive quality or intangible that goes with a 700 score one night, and a 450 the next. You have it, or you don't have it. It comes. It goes. It is being zoned in, and zoned out. It is doing everything just right, or everything just wrong. Timing is coordination of mind and body. Timing is a home run and a golf ball hit 300 yards. It is also a foul ball and a topped shot.

Here are the main points offered by our better bowlers about timing:

Baginski -- "Timing is the most important aspect of bowling. You should be releasing the ball at precisely the same time your slide or plant is ended. If you can do that, you can hit your target with a maximum of action on your ball."

Yeagley -- "I think your timing is everything. If you don't have timing, and you do not feel comfortable, then you can't be consistent. Obviously, if you can't be consistent, you can't get the results you want."

Wolf -- "I find to keep good timing I have to bowl often, not a lot, but often."

Rosenburg -- "For me it is keeping my feet slow, keeping my elbow in and staying down at the line. It is also getting to the line balanced, getting through the ball without jerking up, and staying down and getting through the ball to get pin reaction and good carry."

Duer -- He says his timing is mainly dependent on pushing his ball out at the same time he starts his four-step approach. "If I get to the line with my shoulders square, I am on time."

Campbell -- "The biggest part of timing for me in my five-step approach is the second step when I push the ball away. That's where I work on timing, and that's where I can tell if it's on or off."

AIM/ TARGET

One thing all really good bowlers have in common is the ability to totally focus on a target and hit it.

While bowlers select a variety of targets, including dots, arrows, boards, lines, areas and pins, the best bowlers are renown for consistently hitting their targets.

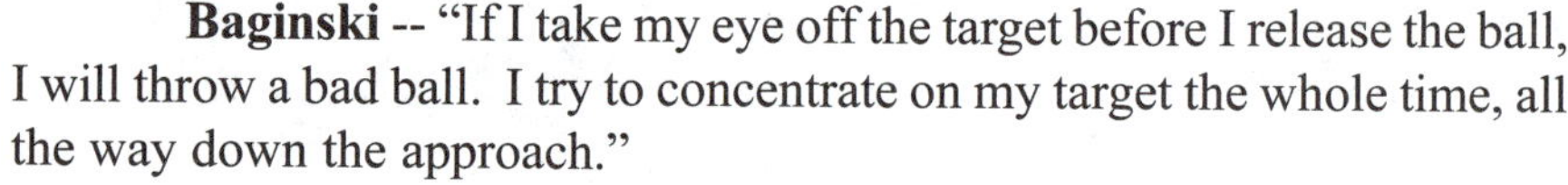

The really great bowlers can place a bowling ball on a crack between boards or roll the ball over the same spot 40 feet down the lane time after time.

Here are the main points offered by our better bowlers about target selection and aiming:

Baginski -- "If I take my eye off the target before I release the ball, I will throw a bad ball. I try to concentrate on my target the whole time, all the way down the approach."

Allan -- "I try to get an idea of how my ball is working on the lanes, and use the boards for my target. I use the dots to line up my feet, and shoot at arrows for strikes and spares. I adjust my target throughout the game, but only when I know I have thrown a good ball and the lanes are changing."

Wolf -- "I like to pick a target about 40 feet down the lane, but I recommend that less experienced bowlers concentrate on using the arrows for a target. It is easier to hit something closer to you, and hitting the target is a psychological boost."

Rosenburg -- "I look at the first row of dots, then down the lane to where I want the ball to go. I draw an imaginary line down the lane to the break point, and throw my ball down that line."

Duer -- "I try to make sure my arm crosses my target, usually a dot, at the foul line and my ball rolls over a targeted dot on the second set of dots and follows a line across a target at the diamonds."

Campbell -- "If I have to focus on a board or target I'll do that, but when I am bowling my best I aim for an area. That gives me more room to hit the pocket."

BACK SWING

Bowling back swings come in all shapes and forms from the tiny, almost no noticeable back swing to the modern power bowlers who are able to bring the ball back and straight up over their heads.

Bowlers and bowling coaches talk about natural back swings, crooked and straight back swings, smooth and jerky back swings, and back swings to increase or lessen ball speed and even hand/arm follow through. Not all bowlers -- including the professionals, coaches and top ranked amateurs -- agree on the importance of the back swing.

Here are the main points offered by our better bowlers on back swings:

Yeagley -- "I try to make sure I keep the ball and the back swing controlled, and that I am not opening my shoulder, that the ball is coming straight back and not behind my back."

Wolf -- "I don't think about the back swing at all. I think it is over rated. The back swing should be natural and contingent on your body structure."

Rosenburg -- "I don't think much about the back swing. I think mine is about normal for what normal people have. I try to be smooth."

Duer -- "The back swing is controlled by where I hold the ball when I start my approach. I hold the ball higher in front of me to get more back swing, and lower the ball to reduce the back swing."

Campbell -- "The back swing is pretty important in my style because it helps me generate the speed I need."

RELEASE

Wrist position and hand position on the ball when it is released determines ball rotation, ball hitting power and pin fall. Basically, the best bowlers keep a stable wrist position for accuracy and consistency and hold a hand position behind and under the ball when it is released. In a sound release the bowler's thumb comes out of the ball first as the bowler follows through the ball with firm finger action. Another important point in release starts with ball fit. The ball should fit well enough that a bowler can hold it with his or her arm extended down toward the approach without having to apply any pressure on the thumb and fingers to keep it from falling. *(See Release Positions at the end of this section.)*

Here are the main points offered by our better bowlers about ball release:

Baginski -- "Keep your ball release as close to your body as you can without hitting your leg or your ankle."

Yeagley -- "My husband always tells me I need to remember to accelerate through the shots and not decelerate. I also try to make sure I keep my hand behind the ball as I come through with it and then rotate it as I come out of it."

Allan -- "Of course you have to be smooth, but a lot of bowlers have the most difficulty in three main areas: staying balanced at the line, keeping their elbow in close to their body and keeping their shoulders square to the target."

Wolf -- "The constant in my release is a firm wrist. You have to have that to be consistent and get rotation on the ball."

Rosenburg -- She cups the ball in her approach and stays behind and under it when she releases it with a firm wrist and a thumb rotation from around 11 o'clock to 10 o'clock.

Duer -- "I hold the ball in the palm of my hand with my thumb facing between 11 and 12 o'clock. When I release the ball my thumb is usually at about 11 o'clock, my wrist is always firm, and I feel the ball go off my fingers."

Blechner -- "I like to get solid fingers into the ball on every shot, and increase the rotation by spreading my index and little fingers wide on the ball." He says you have to have a ball that comes into the pins with a "pow."

LOFT

Loft in bowling refers to the path of the ball in the air immediately after it is released by the bowler. *(See the Loft Section at the end of this section.)*

Here are the main points offered by our better bowlers about loft:

Baginski -- "The loft should be a foot to three feet past the foul line depending on where you finish your slide or plant. The more loft you have, the later the ball will hook down the lane."

Yeagley -- Yeagley does not loft the ball as in throwing it higher than her release point, but throws it long (about six feet out) and low on the lane.

Wolf -- "I recommend that bowlers attempt to get the ball out further, at least a foot or two feet past the foul line to avoid rolling out."

Rosenburg -- Rosenburg does not loft her ball in setting it down four to six inches past the foul line. "I try to keep the ball low."

Duer -- Duer's ball consistently hits the lanes just past the first row of dots past the foul line. He handles roll-out situations with speed, not loft.

Campbell -- "I get additional help in the rotation by delaying the release as long as possible and by getting the ball out on the lanes low and long."

BALL ROTATION

<u>Rotate</u>: To move or turn around a central point or axis. <u>Spin</u>: To rotate without traction. <u>Traction</u>: to grip or hold to a surface while moving without slipping. <u>Revolution</u>: Each time a ball completes one full rotation around the axis, it has made one revolution. To understand ball rotation we have to understand those four definitions.

Basically, a bowling ball rotates, rolls and/or spins in a certain direction on its path or trajectory to a target. Regardless of how a ball is released, it usually spins or slides in the initial phases after its release because most bowling lanes are covered in mineral oil over the first 30 to 40 feet. When the ball eventually grips the lane, it will follow the rotation of the ball. If the rotation is strong and horizontal, the ball will hook. If the rotation is weak, the ball will follow its original path because the force of the throw is stronger than the force of rotation. If the rotation is end-over-end or vertical, it will follow that path.

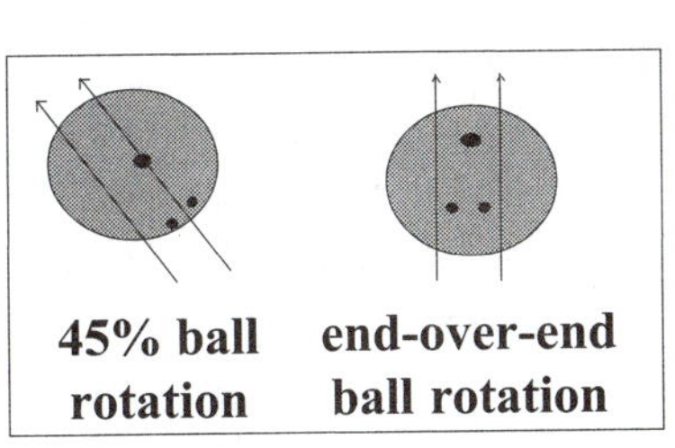

Ball rotation is based on wrist turn at the point of release when by thumb and finger positions the degree (direction) of rotation is determined.

45

Ball revolutions -- combined with speed and angle of the ball into the pocket create hitting power -- are generated by a combination of a firm wrist, firm fingers and follow through. Some 90 percent of all bowlers in the U.S. can be grouped into three categories: The straight-ball bowler, classic bowler and hook-ball bowler. The other 10 percent fall in various categories that include the backup ball and helicopter/spin ball bowlers.

Here are the main points offered by our better bowlers about ball rotation:

Baginski -- "I try to release the ball so it will roll on a right-to-left rotation of about 45 degrees through the oil into the dry area of the lane."

Yeagley -- Yeagley throws a full, or high roller with a flare (ball track) of about two inches.

Rosenburg -- "I try to get a good roll on the ball, and when I do the last thing I feel is the ball on my finger tips."

Duer -- Duer throws a forward roll. "If you get good rotation on the ball it hits harder and carries better."

Campbell -- He says he achieves strong side-to-side rotation on the ball by getting his hand under the ball at his push-away and keeping it there through the back swing and downswing.

FOLLOW THROUGH

The follow through is regarded by nearly every top bowler and coach as the one element in bowling that separates winners from the also-rans.

Follow through actually begins the moment the back swing ends and the bowler's arm and hand begins the forward motion of bringing the ball toward the lanes and a sound position to deliver the ball into the lanes.

The entire sequence of bringing the ball into the lane, releasing the thumb from the ball and pushing the ball onto the lane with your fingers toward a target and continuing the arm and hand motion toward the target after the ball has been released is follow through.

Although individual follow through technique varies from everything to reaching to the ceiling, reaching to the pins and lifting smoothly to every degree of hand-arm angle finish and gunslinger-like drawing actions, the follow through is instrumental in timing, accuracy, ball action and scoring.

Here are the main points offered by our better bowlers about follow through:

Baginski -- "Some people can get away with a short follow through, but generally a good follow through and a good bowler go together." Baginski's follow through brings his hand way over his head.

Yeagley -- "You can have everything else correct -- the timing, the speed -- but if you don't execute the follow through, you will not get the results you need."

Allan -- "Follow through is a must. If you don't have follow through, you are going to throw bowling balls with nothing on them."

STRINGING STRIKES

Bowling two or three consecutive strikes is not that difficult. But as the string gets longer, the degree of difficulty increases for a variety of reasons. Those reasons include: Oil patterns change as bowling balls displace oil and move it from one section to another causing the shot to change. Distractions, mental and physical, mount as the string of strikes grow and bowlers concentrate more on the string rather than on the one shot. Often, when the string reaches four or five or more, many bowlers

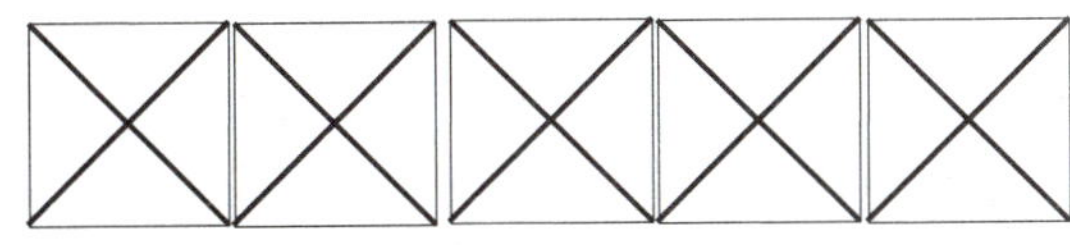

are in new territory and tension mounts, causing muscle tightness and a loss of the ease and smooth delivery the bowler had when the string began. Finally, as the string grows bowlers have a tendency to try harder, which often results in flattening the ball -- aiming rather than rolling -- and pulled shots from trying to put "just a little more" on the ball.

Here are the main points offered by our better bowlers about stringing strikes:

Baginski -- "Some people can't string strikes because as soon as they throw a couple they start thinking about it too much. I play one ball at a time, and try not to think about a string."

Yeagley -- "I focus on one good shot at a time. I work at it one frame at a time."

Wolf -- "I try to throw the best shot I can every time, and if I am lucky I throw eight or nine perfect shots a night."

Rosenburg -- "I don't think about the three or four in a row. I think one frame and one ball at a time."

Duer -- "When I get up to bowl I just concentrate on hitting the mark."

Campbell -- "When I'm stringing strikes I look at every frame as a new frame, focusing on the task at hand rather than what has happened."

SPARES

Making spares is often not given as much consideration as it should in the overall game of bowling. The good bowlers practice making spares and make most of them. The excellent bowlers almost never miss a spare because they know "if you make your spares, the strikes will come." A bowler can hit a 190 game without a strike. Hall of Fame bowler Joe Wilman said in his 1953 book *Better Bowling* that "making spares consistently is the principal distinction between the star and the average bowler." That is still true today. But unlike those days, many good bowlers today with hooks and curves usually use a plastic ball to convert spares with straight shots. Here are the main points offered by our better bowlers about making spares:

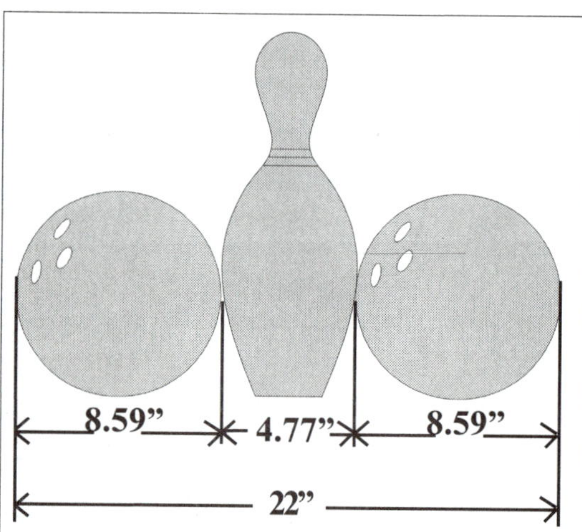

SPARE ROOM -- Bowlers have nearly a 22-inch target (more than half a lane) when converting a one-pin spare. Pins are 4.77 inches wide, and bowling balls are 8.59 inches wide. The ball can hit the pin, even a 7 or 10 pin, from either side.

Wolf -- He throws a thumb-first straight ball for spares. His spare ball is a very old 16-pound Brunswick Mineralite.

Rosenburg -- "I just use my weakest hooking ball." She throws a flattened straight ball from the left and right corners for the 10 and 7 pins, and throws a small hook for all other spares.

Duer -- "I don't look at the pins. I just know what spot I want to throw the ball over to hit a particular pin." He does not change balls for spares.

Blechner -- He uses the

same ball for strikes and spares. "I shoot all the spares except the 10-pin exactly as I throw the strike ball." He throws a cross-lane ball with more speed and less lift to convert the 10 pin.

Campbell -- He throws a straight shot to convert spares. "I use my weakest ball, and flatten it out."

PRACTICE

The actual amount of practice the best bowlers accomplish varies a great deal, as does the way they practice. The only constant is that the best bowlers have put in the time to learn how to bowl, have learned how to practice and bowl often in league and tournament competition.

> **OPEN BOWLING**
> **9 A.M. TO 4 P.M. M-F**
> **11 A.M. TO 11 P.M. S-S**

The best bowlers have a sound understanding of bowling fundamentals. They understand technique, know how to adjust for spare conversions and lane conditions, and keep up to date in their knowledge of bowling equipment.
Here are the main points offered by our better bowlers about practice:

Baginski -- "Work on one thing at a time. Don't worry about your practice scores because the practice scores don't mean anything. Always work on your timing."

McManus -- "Bowlers always get a period for practice before league bowling begins. Use the time wisely. Throw a couple of balls just to warm up, then take a shot at a 7 pin, 10 pin, a 6 and a 4. When you do that you not only get ready for spares, you find out how much oil is on the lane by checking the action of your ball."

Yeagley -- "I pick up the bowling ball and swing it around a little, trying to stretch my arms and loosen my back before actually throwing a ball. I also do some bending and get my mind set on bowling."

Wolf -- "When I practice I work on a single shot and try to see how many times I can throw the same shot."

Duer -- Duer bowls in five leagues and a number of tournaments throughout the year, so he does not often schedule a practice session.

MENTAL GAME

The term "mentally tough" is not just a cliche`. Mentally tough in bowling means having the ability to focus on an objective and maintain that focus despite a myriad of mental and physical distractions.

The best athletes make the free throw, kick the field goal, hit the

ball and throw the strike when the game is on the line. Mental toughness often is the difference between success and failure. A lack of mental toughness separates gifted amateur athletes from professionals.

Here are the main points offered by our better bowlers on the mental game:

Baginski -- "I just take one ball at a time. I have the same routine every time. I get up there, dry my hands, wipe my ball off and think about throwing a strike.

Yeagley -- "I tell myself to focus on one frame at a time. I can't do anything about the frames that have happened, and I can't do anything about the frames that haven't happened, so I focus on now."

Wolf -- "Don't try to think of too many things when you are on the approach. Concentrate on just doing one or two things perfectly."

Rosenburg -- "For me the mental game is thinking about what I need to do."

Duer -- "My mental approach is to think I can knock all the pins down all the time. You gotta believe you can do that or you might as well not go down there."

Campbell -- "You have to screen out the highs and lows. If you let yourself get too high, than all you are doing is setting yourself up to crash. You have to be able to maintain a certain focus."

Fast Facts

Chris Barnes, Flower Mound, Texas, by way of Wichita State University in Kansas, was PBA Rookie of the Year in 1998. Other top rookies that year were Wayne Guernsey of Cobleskill, N.Y., Patrick Healey Jr. of Taylor, Mich., Jason Hurd of Visalia, Calif., Robert Morton of Boulder Junction, Colo., Curt Pilon of Clinton Township, Mich., Robert Smith of Moorpark, Calif., Sean Swanson of Springfield, Mo., and Lee Vanderhoef of Rising Sun, Md.

RELEASE POSITIONS

Hand position on the ball when it is released is very important in setting the ball rotation, ball hitting power and pin fall. While there are many release positions, those most often used include these four main positions:

A. When the ball is released from the suitcase position bowlers usually release the thumb and fingers at the same time. The ball has little rotation, and consequently little hitting power. Another fault of the "suitcase" delivery is many bowlers drop the ball from this position. Ball rotation can be increased by releasing the thumb just ahead of the fingers, and lifting with the fingers in a sound follow through.

B. Staying under the ball during the approach allows the bowler to get his or her thumb out of the ball first, and rotate the ball toward the pins by applying good finger lift in the release follow through. This action usually results in a full-roller hook.

C. Bowlers have the best opportunity to let the ball do the work with a hand position behind the ball. From behind the ball it is easier to get your thumb out first and let the natural follow through give the ball good roll.

D. Behind the ball, but with more side rotation imparts side roll on the ball and a longer, curving path to the pins when releasing the thumb first and lifting with the fingers in the follow through.

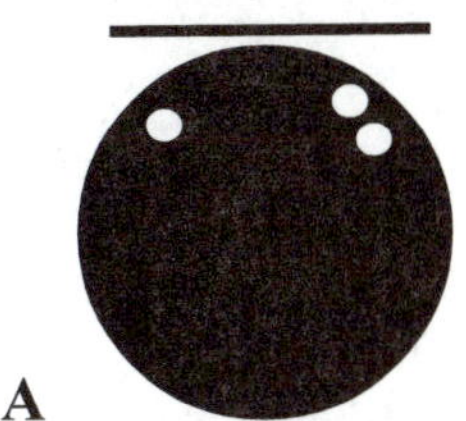

A

On Top of the Ball. "Suitcase."

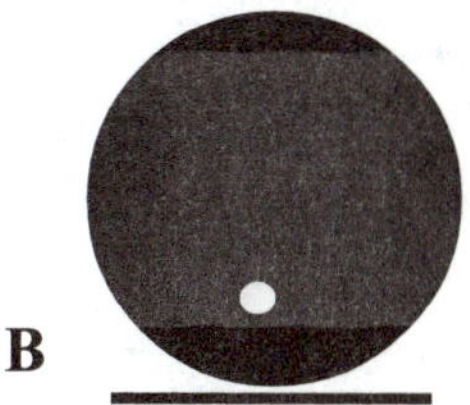

B

Under the Ball

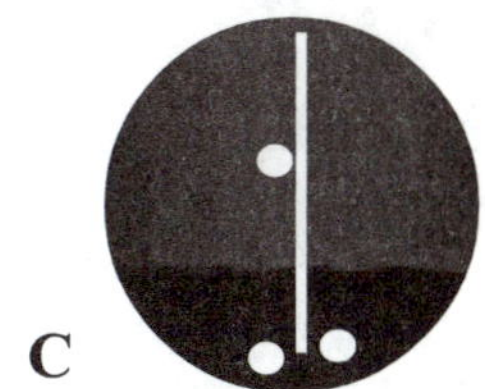

C

Behind the Ball

D

On the side of the Ball

LOFT

Loft in bowling refers to the path of the ball in the air immediately after it is released by the bowler.

Is it important?

Most top bowlers say it is very important and has a great deal to do with success or failure. The way the ball is delivered to the lane impacts a bowler's timing, revolutions of the ball, breaking point of a hook or curve ball, path of the ball and ball speed. Another very important element in bowling that is impacted by loft is the bowler's follow through.

First, it should be explained that there is no one perfect method of lofting the ball. Bowlers are successful with very short lofts, lofts of up to four or five feet, lofts that cause the ball to make noise when it hits the lanes, and lofts that are so smooth and even with the lanes -- much like the smooth landing of an airplane -- that there is no noise at all when the ball flows into the lane.

Bowling coach John Jowdy, in his book *Bowling Execution*, recommends a "long and low" loft and says bowlers can practice achieving the ideal loft by pretending to deliver the ball into the lane under a one foot high bar. (See Fig. L-1)

In many ways the term "loft" is misused. It does NOT mean the ball has to go up after it is delivered as a softball arcs when it is delivered

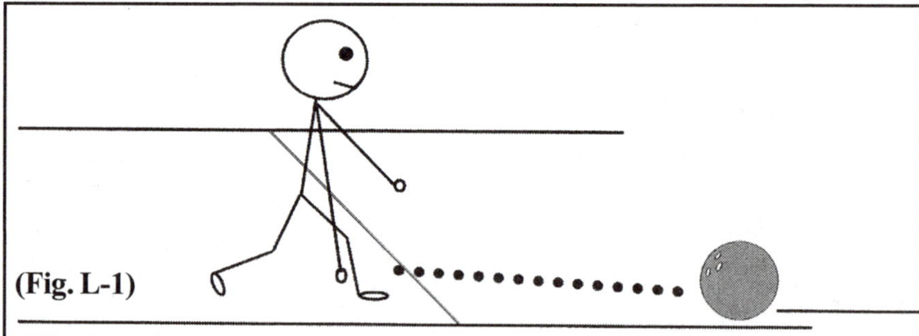

(Fig. L-1)

The long, low loft is recommended because it gets the ball into the lane smoothly, and allows the bowler the best possibility for a sound follow through.

(Fig. L-2)

While loft distance varies considerably from bowler to bowler, the average is from six to 18 inches beyond the foul line.

by a pitcher in slow-pitch softball. Instead, loft means the distance the ball travels from the bowler's hand to the lanes.

The average loft distance by top bowlers is around six inches to about 18 inches -- three feet would be a maximum -- beyond the foul line. It is achieved by throwing the ball out toward a target. (Fig. L-2) Many bowlers vary the distance of the loft in order to control the breaking point of the hook and/or curve ball further down the lane. By getting more loft, bowlers start the ball rolling later, and delaying the hooking/curving action. Bowlers who want the ball to hook or curve earlier often set the ball down closer to the foul line.

The two types of deliveries that should be avoided are the extremes of dropping the ball and throwing it on an upward trajectory. In both cases the ball slams to the floor and damages the lanes. (Fig. L-3 and

(Fig. L-3)

Dropping the ball is usually caused by releasing the thumb and fingers from the ball at the same time from a position on top of the ball. Too, some bowlers simply drop the ball -- like a hot potato -- rather than placing it smoothly on the lane.

Fig. L-4) Many bowling centers post signs reminding bowlers "Do Not Loft the Ball." Most bowling centers ban bowlers who damage the lanes. Dropped balls, which result in little or no action when they hit the pins, are usually caused by releasing the thumb and fingers from the ball at the same time from a position on top of the ball. That position is often referred to as the "suitcase" position. One other main reason bowler's drop the ball is an inability to bend at the knees. In those cases bowlers can eliminate the "straight-down" trajectory by throwing the ball further out on the lane or simply bending at the waist to get the ball closer to the lane surface.

While there are many, many strange bowling styles in bowling centers around the world, the oddity that gets the most attention is the bowler

The high trajectory ball that hits the lanes with a loud thud can do a lot of damage. Bowlers who regularly throw the loud thuds are not welcome in bowling centers.

who throws the ball into the air for some distance only to watch (and hear) it hit the lane in a trajectory similar to a diving pelican. That kind of ball can do a lot of damage to the lanes, and unless the bowler who throws it owns the lanes or is a dear relative of the owner he or she is not going to be welcome in the bowling center.

A good rule of thumb in bowling pertaining to loft and/or any other elements in bowling is if your technique is very unusual and your scores are not so good, you probably should look at what bowlers around you are doing and see if maybe, just maybe you might improve your bowling by dropping the unusual and being a bit more like the bowler with the 200+ average.

LANE CONDITIONS

Oil. Oil. Oil.

When most bowlers talk about lane conditions, they are really talking about how much or how little oil has been applied to the lanes. Oil is the difference between a "fast" lane and a "slow" lane. Oil is often the difference between a ball that hooks into the pocket with authority, and one that fades off the head pin with as much punch as a blade of grass. Except in cases where lanes are uneven, worn out or are poorly maintained, the major differences from one lane to the other -- even including wood and synthetic lanes -- is the amount of oil on them.

Basically, bowling lanes are coated in a type of mineral oil from the foul line to about 15 or 20 feet in front of the pins to protect them from the pounding they get from bowling balls. It's said that a 16-pound bowling ball hits the lane with a force of around 2000 pounds per square inch. So, to protect the lanes, oil is applied so a thrown ball will skid when it hits the lanes.

Lane owners have computerized equipment to apply the oil in a number of

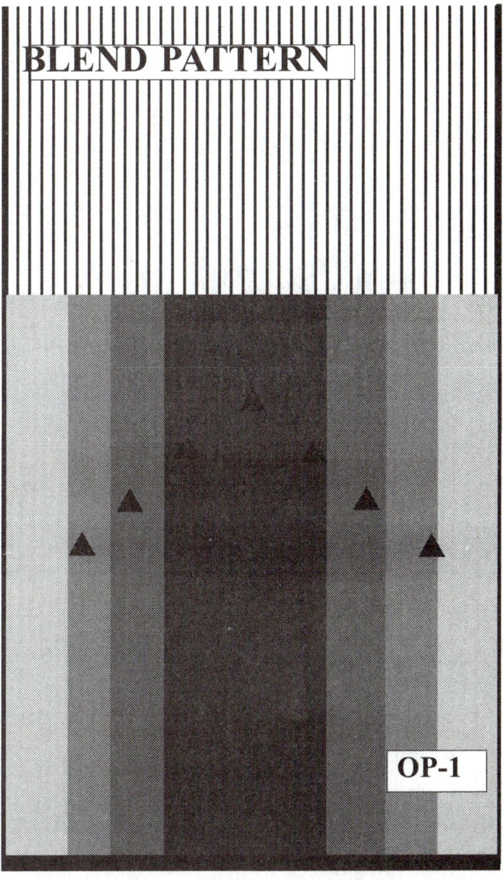

BLEND PATTERN -- In the blend pattern, the most common oil pattern league bowlers encounter in bowling centers across the country, the oil is applied at the same length down the lane -- usually around 35 feet -- with the heaviest oil on the center 20 boards (darkest). The least amount of oil is applied to the outside five boards (lightest) on both sides of the lane.

patterns, but the patterns most used in bowling centers during league competition are the "blend" (see fig. OP-1), the "Christmas tree" (see fig. OP-2), and "block." (see fig. OP-3). A "flat" pattern (see fig. OP-4) with the oil applied evenly over all boards down the lane to 30 or 35 feet is a pattern operators often use for tournament competition.

In professional competition and sport bowling, the patterns are dictated by the Professional Bowlers Association and United States Bowling Congress rules. Those patterns are designed to make bowling much more difficult than league and recreational bowlers face.

In most bowling centers for league competition and practice bowling most of the oil is applied where most of the balls are first thrown, and that is in the middle of the lane from the 10th board on the right to the 10th board from the left. There also is oil on the edges of the lanes, but not as much as in the middle.

CHRISTMAS TREE -- The oil pattern is very similar to the blend pattern, but the outside boards are oiled very lightly and the three inside patterns are staggered in length. This pattern tends to favor the hook-ball bowlers who can throw across the oil pattern in a variety of targets and bring the ball back into the headpin from as far out as right of the five board to as tight as the 15 board.

Balls thrown normally with a normal amount of speed on the oiled sections of the lane skid more than they roll. So good bowlers actually try to skid/roll the ball down the lane to the dry section where they hope the rotation they put on the ball will take affect and the ball will roll into the pocket of the pins with a driving impact.

High average bowlers practice throwing the ball through the oil area to the dry area so it will begin to roll, sometimes curving and sometimes hooking, at just the right break point to hit the pins at precisely the place where the ball is at maximum grip and maximum rotation.

Oil is colorless and nearly impossible to see, although some veterans claim they can tell where the oil is by where the lane is dull and where there is a glassiness.

Most bowlers try to figure out the oil pattern during pre-league practice balls. Watch your ball and watch others to see where the balls begin to break toward the head pin. That will tell you how far down the lane the oil has been applied. Balls breaking early indicate a short oil pattern, while balls that break just in front of the pins indicates a long oil pattern.

The 10 pins in total weigh between 36 and 37 pounds, so if a bowler is going to consistently throw strikes, the ball has to have impact to roll through those pins without being deflected

BLOCK -- The block pattern with consistent oil across the center 30 boards and little oil on the outside five boards is also a common oil pattern for league bowling. The oil on the center boards allows for all kinds of bowling shots, while the lack of oil on the outside boards will aid in keeping balls revolving toward the headpin from slipping into the gutter. The dry area is called the block .

FLAT -- The flat pattern with an even distribution of oil across all the boards down the lane 30 to 35 feet was a common pattern used for tournament bowling but not used much since the 2000s.

too much to the right or left of the middle five pin.

A sliding ball or one with little rotation has little impact and is deflected away from the head pin and the key five pin in the middle of the set.

Another problem with all of this is that the oil does not stay where it was first applied. Bowling balls pick up the oil and carry it into the dry areas. That does two things. It drys the oil area, and oils the dry area. As a result, balls that hit a dry area sooner start to roll sooner, resulting in an eventual loss of ball revolutions and ball hitting power.

Balls thrown on lanes where the oil has "carried down" skid longer, and do not hit the pins at maximum rotation. A skidding ball, much like an automobile on ice, has no grip.

Bottom line?

Figuring out lane conditions and how to play them plays a major role in separating the professional bowler and the high average bowlers from the rest.

Fast Facts

How many bowling centers and lanes are there in the United States? According to the United States Bowling Congress, 5,646 centers were certified in the 2004-2005 season. With an average of 20.46 lanes per center, there are 115,704 lanes in the United States.

GETTING READY TO BOWL

Getting ready to bowl is one of the most important aspects of bowling, yet, it is also the most neglected single area of bowling. People have a tendency to rush to the lanes, put on bowling shoes, grab a ball and start firing. That scenario fits beginners, practice situations and league bowlers alike. It doesn't, however, fit professionals because they know how important it is to <u>mentally prepare for the game</u>, <u>warm up by stretching a few muscles</u> and <u>check out their bowling equipment</u>.

Mental Game: Put all your other worries aside for a few moments and focus on where you are and what you need to do. Are you loose and is your equipment ready? How are your teammates doing?   What are the lane conditions? How much adjusting will you have to do? How many bowlers appear to be shooting the same line you do? Are there any bowlers on the other team who could distract me when I'm bowling because they linger at the line or rush to bowl without checking adjoining lanes? Are you ready to focus on your target? Am I ready to bowl?

Checking Your Equipment: Every once in a while a bowler walks down the approach to throw his or her first ball, slides and falls head-first down the lane. That usually happens because of a dirty approach or dirty sliding shoe sole.   It is always a good idea to <u>check the bottom of your shoes</u> before you put them on to see if they are clean. A piece of candy or some other sticky substance on a sliding shoe can cause big problems. If you do find something on the shoe, clean it off. Now, without the ball, <u>check your lanes for slide</u>. Are they sticky? Are they slippery? Be sure about your shoes and the lanes before you throw that first ball.

Also <u>check your bowling ball</u> to make sure it is reasonably clean and ready. <u>Check the surface and the finger and thumb holes</u>. A glob of oil or some other substance on the ball will give your ball some strange reactions. Fingers and thumbs have a tendency to shrink and swell. Does the ball fit well, or do you need an insert or two to tighten a hole, or a little powder to be sure you get out of the ball okay. One of the worst accidents in bowling after falling down can occur if the ball sticks to your fingers or thumb.

Check your <u>clothing and your jewelry</u> to make sure they fit comfortably and you can't snag on them in any way while you are bowling.

Warm-up and Stretching: Everyone is a little bit different when it comes to strength and muscles, but one thing is certain, it is always a good idea to warm up and stretch your muscles before starting any strenuous activity, including throwing a 10- to 16-pound ball around. Here are a few general stretching exercises. Combine these with some activity such as walking around the block to increase blood circulation, getting lose with your practice throws, and you will be ready to bowl. Don't try to do too much at first. You can gradually increase the activity over time.

Hamstring Stretch - Place the heel of the leg being stretched on a box or bench about knee high. Keep your hips facing forward. Keep your leg straight on the bench and lean forward toward your toe gently and firmly. Keep you back straight. Get to the point of stretch, and hold it for about 10 seconds. Repeat that for each leg at least twice. (The hamstring is the large muscle behind the thigh and a tight hamstring is a leading cause of lower back pain.) You can also stretch the hamstring while sitting, placing you foot on a step and leaning forward, standing with one leg placed far in front of the other and bending forward.

Quadriceps Stretch - Clasp your foot behind your body with your hand. Pull your foot upward, and push your bent knee forward. You should have your free hand on a fence or something solid to give you balance and keep you from falling. Stretch the quadriceps (the four muscles in front of your thigh) gently, and hold the stretch about 10 seconds. Repeat for each leg at least twice.

Neck Stretch - Tuck your head forward as much as you can. Now gently and slowly twist your head to the left as far as you can. Hold that position for a few seconds. Now look to the right twisting your head in that direction as far as you can. Hold that position for a few seconds. Repeat this several times, staying gentle and firm, for best results in stretching the neck muscles.

Lower Back and Stomach Stretch - Stand straight. Fold your arms in front of your stomach. Gently turn your torso (upper body) as far to the left as you can without allowing your hips to turn. When you get as far to the left as you can, hold the position for a few seconds. Repeat the motion going to the right. Repeat both actions several times to stretch your lower back and stomach muscles.

Other Areas - You might also stretch your forearms, your hands, calf and chest muscles, all areas important in bowling. Your routine and the amount of stretching you do depends on your health and ability. Don't overdo it, but don't neglect this important part of bowling and staying fit.

STRATEGIES IN BOWLING

Team

Math! Everything in this world really does come down to math. Team success or failure can be determined in large part on how one team matches up mathematically against other teams.

High average teams in handicap leagues where the handicap is less than 100 percent stand the best chance of winning for two main reasons:

First, if the handicap is based on 90 percent or 80 percent, the highest average bowler has a 10 or 20 percent advantage.

Second, if a bowler is above the handicap standard -- the standard is usually anywhere from 190 to 220 --- that bowler actually is given "free" pins for any pins above the standard average. A 210 average bowler in a league with a standard of 200 gets zero handicap, but is given 10 free pins per game because the 10 pins above the standard are not figured against him or her.

The highest average teams in scratch leagues also stand the best chance of winning. Why? The answer is easy. Knowing that on any given night almost any bowler can defeat almost any other bowler, the law of

Score Sheet						
Average	Bowler's Name	Hcp.	1	2	3	
196	Bill　　LEADOFF　—	13				
184	Ron　　SECOND	23				
179	Hank　　MIDDLE　—	28				
187	Gary　　FOURTH　—	21				
219	Mike　　ANCHOR　—	0				
	Substitute					

•**Leadoff is usually the team's second best bowler and one capable of setting a tone for the rest of the team.**
•**Second is usually the team's fourth best bowler.**
•**Middle spot is usually the lowest average bowler on the team.**
•**Fourth is usually the team's third best bowler and one capable of scoring well in the clutch.**
•**Anchor is usually the team's best bowler and one most dependable, especially when the game is close.**

averages always gets its due. A 210 bowler -- not one who is erratic with 240s and 180s, but one who is fairly consistent --- will beat the 205 or less bowler most of the time simply because of the average fact that the 210 bowler hits 210, while the 205 bowler hits 205. Average is, after all, the ruling factor.

Team strategy also plays a role in how a team places its bowlers.

The highest average bowler usually bowls last in the order -- the anchor spot -- because he or she is expected to come through most often in the final frames of games that are close. Some of the high average bowlers, however, prefer not to bowl in the anchor spot for a variety of reasons, including not being able to handle pressure.

A team's leadoff bowler is usually the second best bowler on the team and can be depended on to get the team going and set a good example.

Individual Strategy

Compared to other sports, there isn't much strategy in the game of bowling an individual bowler has to consider that is ethical or legal.

Good bowlers simply strive to bowl the best they can in league and tournament competition. The best bowlers try not to be influenced by the competition in that they concentrate on their own game.

Bowlers who are improving, and bowl better than their early-season averages, have advantages in the latter stages of a season, and can get an advantage in tournaments where older averages are used.

On the unethical or illegal side there are some individual strategies bowlers should know about. Yes, Virginia, there are some bowlers called "sandbaggers" who hold their averages down to gain advantages in tournaments and league competition --take note of the bowlers who suddenly miss spares and head pins when their scores are not needed.

Watch out, too, for the bowler who last year averaged 200+, and in first part of the new season averages just enough for his or her team to win.   That's the bowler who is showing signs of sandbagging to get an advantage in the second half of the season and in tournaments.

Consistency is the key to winning and is a strategy worth striving to achieve. Individual bowlers who can consistently bowl a few pins better than their average each game will win the majority of the time while developing a technique they can count on from night to night, lane to lane, and center to center.

The experts say that bowlers do best if they stay "within themselves." That means if you understand your skills and weaknesses and bowl within those perimeters -- not trying to throw wild hooks with a weak wrist or straight balls when you have a nice, natural curve --- you will consistently bowl well, and better.

Another so-called strategy -- it falls in the poor sportsmanship category -- is the practice of trash talk and visual interference.

First, the visual interference. It is not always an accident when bowlers, especially from the other team, race down the approach to get a shot off while you are focusing on a key spare or strike shot. If you are not able to totally concentrate because of the distraction -- and most bowlers, even the pros, are not -- your best bet is to wait out that bowler and let them bowl first, or at least let them know you know he or she is there.

Trash talk comes in a variety of forms, including sweet talk such as "you really had that ball rotating on that strike" -- and all of it is geared to get you to lose concentration. "Wow," you say, "I really did have that ball rotating on that strike. On the next one I'll rotate it even more." Guess what happens on the next one?

Compliments are good and welcome, but talk about your technique is usually a call for "distraction."

Fast Facts

The **Budweiser Team of St. Louis** held the five-man team total record of 3,858 for nearly 36 years. All five members of that team, **Don Carter**, **Ray Bluth**, **Pat Patterson**, **Tom Hennessey** and **Dick Weber**, became members of bowling's Hall of Fame.

They set the record March 12, 1958, at Floriss Lanes, a 16-lane center in St. Louis, on games of 1,265, 1,300 and 1,293. Carter rolled 754 on games of 266, 253 and 235. Bluth followed with the highest score, an 834 on 267, 267 and 300. Patterson had the lowest score, a 736 on 246, 222 and 268. Hennessey hit 759 on 228, 300 and 231. Weber had 775 on a near triplicate of 258, 258 and 259. For the entire night the team had 138 strikes out of a possible 180 and registered only four open frames, two missed splits and two missed 10 pins.

Their record was first broken by **Hurst Bowling Supplies** of Luzerne, Pa., with a 3,868 on Feb. 23, 1994. The current record of 3,934 was set by **Limo Exchange** in New Castle, Del., April 1, 2004.

BOWLING'S QUESTIONS & ANSWERS

❖*How much should I practice?* Some bowlers practice very little and seem to do okay. Most of the best bowlers, however, bowl in at least two leagues and practice once or twice a week. Most professionals practice at least an hour a day, and bowl in several leagues and a lot of tournaments. The only rule of thumb is "practice makes perfect." Most bowling centers post their open bowling schedules. Some centers give discounts to league bowlers.

❖*How do I determine the correct ball weight for me?* Seek help on this one from a professional coach, the pro-shop operator or an experienced better bowler who knows your game. The bottom line for you is does the ball feel comfortable. Can you get proper loft on the ball (be able to throw it a foot to a foot and a half beyond the four line) and not lose your balance or grip on the ball. The proper fit of the ball has a lot to do with how much weight a bowler can handle.

❖*How can I throw a hook ball?* A lot of bowlers, young and old, ask that question, and a lot of bowlers try to answer it by last minute wrist turns and other jerky methods to impart spin on the bowling ball. Hook balls and curve balls are thrown by getting your hand under the ball at delivery, and imparting horizontal rotation (right to left for a right handed bowler and left to right for a left handed bowler) when the ball is released. Bowlers with a lot of action on the ball get good lift on the ball and demonstrate a good follow through (going through the ball) when they finish the release. Why do you want a hook or curve?   Bowlers who throw hooks and curves have two big advantages. First, a good hook/curve ball has good rotation, and that contributes to greater pin action. Second, balls entering the pocket at sharper angles also get better mix, and thus more strikes and higher scores.

❖*How do you get on a league bowling team?* Most bowling centers will keep a list of people interested in bowling on a team. Team captains who need players usually check with the centers. Another way to get on a team is to simply show up at the lanes opening night or day or any time league play is scheduled and check around to see if any team needs a bowler.

If you don't find a team at first, keep trying because team personnel changes during the season due to a variety of reasons.

A word of caution! Don't just get on ANY team. If you are going to enjoy bowling, it really helps to bowl with people you can like and enjoy. Before you join a league or team you might want to find out a little about the averages in the league to see if you are compatible and competitive. You also should find out about the bowlers (ask bowling center people who know most of the bowlers) to see if they are "your kind of people." Some bowlers are "for-fun" bowlers, while some are very serious, and most are a little of both. Finally, be sure the league schedule which is usually around 32 to 36 weeks fits your schedule. When you join a team you are expected to be on time, not miss many matches, and pay the league fee every week.

❖*Should I join the United States Bowling Congress?* The USBC is the sanctioning body of bowling. Most leagues in the United States require bowlers to join the USBC for a number of reasons: 1. Only scores bowled in sanctioned leagues are recognized in the record books. 2. Most tournaments require bowlers to be USBC members. 3. The USBC establishes and maintains rules and equipment regulations that help keep bowling fair to all bowlers.

❖*Will bowling centers repair or replace my ball if it is damaged while bowling there?* A lot depends on how the ball was damaged, the extent of the damage, and if the damage was clearly caused by something on the lanes and no fault of the bowler. If the center is clearly at fault, most centers will repair and sometimes replace the ball. Being timely about reporting the damage is also important. If your ball is damaged, report it immediately. A good time to spot damage is when you wipe off your ball before starting your frame. By reporting ball damage as soon as it happens you also help lane management find the cause and fix it.

❖*Where can I get some help learning how to bowl?* Check with the people running the bowling center. They can usually get you lined up with United States Bowling Congress coaches or some of the better bowlers in the center. If you are a beginning bowler, the sooner you get help the sooner you will be hitting higher scores, and you will not have to get rid of some bad habits. Few bowlers start out as good bowlers. If you have been bowling for a while and you want to get better, you, too, should check with the bowling center and get some good coaching help. A good coach can spot your mistakes and help you improve.

BOWLING'S HISTORY

Writers have envisioned and written a variety of bowling histories in a variety of publications over the past 100 years or so. The truth is no one knows where or when bowling was born. Bowling has simply evolved and it continues to evolve as new equipment and new methods are found and used. Cavemen and cavewomen, looking for an entertaining way to compliment a day of hunting and being hunted, probably at some time some place rolled an object – it could have been a stone, a small pumpkin, or anything you can think of that would roll fairly well – into other objects to hit them or knock them down. And even that probably evolved from a time when some cave person without thought rolled something at something and said "oh, that's fun. I wonder if I can do that again."

Bowling as we know it with 10 pins weighing no less than 3 pounds, a lane 60 feet long and 41 to 42 inches wide, a bowling ball weighing no more than 16 pounds, 10 frames and a possible score of 300 really began in 1895 when the American Bowling Congress was founded in New York City to write rules and make the game uniform.

In the early days of bowling the lanes and bowling establishments were called "allies" and they were mostly placed either under or above "legitimate" businesses. The bowling centers were in the same category as early-age, back-street pool halls and often harbored the "rough and tough" and contributed greatly to "misspent youth." Eventually bowling caught on with women – the Women's International Bowling Congress was founded in 1917 – and bowling establishments spruced up and welcomed the females.

Bigger, better, bowling establishments were constructed in the 1950s. Pin boys who had been setting the 10 pins and returning the bowling balls were being replaced by machines, fouls were watched and called by electronic eye instead of the human eye, many of the very best bowlers joined newly formed professional ranks, and more and more people learned how to bowl and joined local bowling leagues. The early television shows that included Fred Wolf's "Championship Bowling," "Make that Spare," "Bowling for Dollars," and "Celebrity Bowling" contributed a great deal to the growing popularity of the sport. In 1961 the ABC Television Network offered its first coverage of the Pro Bowlers tour, enhancing bowling popularity and making the names of Dick Weber, Don Carter, Carmen Salvino, Bob Strampe, Ray Bluth, Junie McMahon, Billy Welu and "Wrong Foot" Lou Campi known to bowlers everywhere.

Today there are an estimated 95 million bowlers in 90 countries including 50 million bowlers in the United States, and 6 million of those compete in leagues and tournaments in all 50 states. According to the United States Bowling Congress, there are more than 6,000 bowling establishments with more than 125,000 lanes in the U.S., and another 4,000 establishments outside the U.S. with an additional 75,000 lanes. Sales of bowling products total more than $220 million annually.

More people participate in bowling in the United States than in any other sport. Bowling is open to the young and the old, the fit and the infirm and hosts leagues for bowlers of all skill levels. Baseball may be America's pastime, but bowling is America's participant prime-time.

THE GAME

The object of the game of bowling is to knock down as many pins as possible using the fewest number of shots. A game consists of 10 individual frames. In each frame the bowler faces a set of 10 pins. A bowler has two shots to knock down the 10 pins in each frame. Knocking down the 10 pins on the first shot is a strike. A strike is the ideal shot, and it is scored as 10 plus whatever the bowler can score on his or her next two shots in the next frame or next two 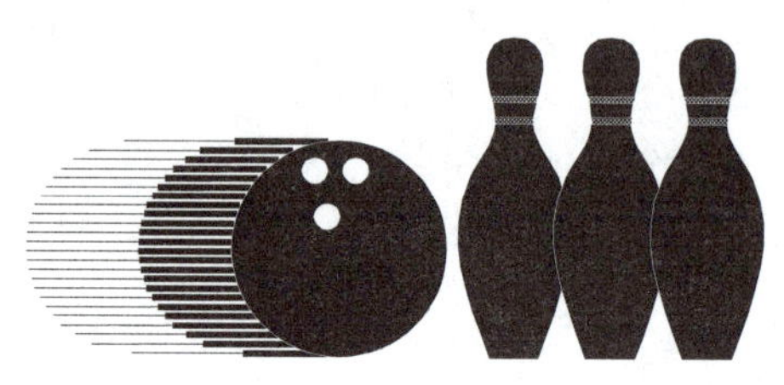 frames if the bowler continues to throw strikes. It is possible to score 30 pins in a single frame. If the bowler does not knock down all the pins on the first shot, the bowler throws a second shot to knock down the pins. If successful, that is a spare. A spare is scored as 10 pins plus whatever pins the bowler knocks down on the very next ball in the next frame. It is

 possible to score 20 pins on a spare. If the bowler does not knock down all the pins in a single frame, that is called a miss, and the bowler gets a score in that frame equal to the number of pins knocked down. The 10th frame, the last frame of the game, is different from the other frames. In the 10th frame the bowler may shoot as many as three times. In the 10th frame if the bowler gets a strike, the bowler has the chance to shoot at another set of 10 pins and may get another strike, in which case the bowler is awarded a third ball to shoot at another set of 10 pins and complete the game. If the bowler does not get a strike on the first ball, the bowler has a second ball to try to knock down all the pins for a spare. If successful, the bowler has to deliver a third shot at a new set of 10 pins to complete the scoring and the game. If a bowler records a miss in the 10th frame, the bowler's game is finished and he or she does not get a third ball. Bowling scores range from less than 100 to 300 for a perfect score of 12 straight strikes. While a bowler shoots at just 10 pins in each of the first nine frames and a possible 30 pins in the 10th frame, a total of 120 pins, extra pins are awarded for recording strikes and spares.

KEEPING SCORE

In order to keep score, bowlers should know that a game consists of 10 frames (turns). In each of the first nine frames bowlers are allowed two shots to knock down the 10 pins. The tenth frame is special, and we will discuss that later. The only "tricky" part in keeping score, and the part that is most confusing at first, is figuring scores on spares and strikes.

Spares are noted on the score sheet by a slash in the small box in the right upper corner of the score sheet. To get a spare a bowler has to knock down all ten pins in the frame in two shots. A spare counts 10 pins plus the number of pins the bowler knocks down on the next shot after the spare. (This will be easier to understand in the following score sheet example/explanation.)

Strikes are noted on the score sheet by an X in the small box in the right upper corner of the score sheet. A bowler registers a strike when all 10 pins are knocked down on the first ball. A strike counts 10 pins plus the number of pins knocked down on the bowler's next two shots. (This will be easier to understand in the following score sheet example/ explanation.)

Bowlers are allowed two shots to get all 10 pins in each of the first nine frames. In the 10th frame bowlers may get a third ball to complete the scoring for a spare or strike in the frame. A third ball is awarded if a

NAME	1	2	3	4	5	6	7	8	9	10
	9 /	X	⑧ –	7 /	X	X	9 –	F /	X	6 / 8
Ron McIntosh	20	38	46	66	95	114	123	143	163	181

bowler gets a spare or two strikes on the first two balls. If the bowler misses the spare, the bowler does not get a third ball.

Here is an actual, frame-by-frame example of how to score a game.

First frame: Ron got nine pins on his first ball. A score of nine is noted in the area left of the small mark box in the larger scoring box. He knocked down the pin on the second ball for a spare. The spare is noted by the slash in the mark box. **Second frame**: Ron threw a strike. The first-frame spare counted 10 pins plus the total of the next ball, so 10 plus 10 is 20 for the first frame. The strike is noted with an X in the mark box. **Third frame**: Ron hit the head pin pretty full, and left the dreaded 7-10 split. An 8 is registered on the sheet, the split is noted by a circle around the 8. Ron missed both pins on his second shot. Because he had a strike in the second frame, the score could not be filled out until after he completed his second ball after the strike. In this case he got eight pins, so eight is added to the spare-strike total of 30 pins in the second frame, plus eight pins in the third frame for a total of 46. **Fourth frame**: Ron got seven pins on his first shot. He knocked down the remaining three pins for a spare. **Fifth frame**: Ron threw a strike. Strikes count 10 plus the number of pins knocked down on the next two balls. **Sixth frame**: Ron threw another strike. **Seventh frame**: Ron got nine pins on his first ball. A nine is recorded and nine pins are added to the fifth frame total because the shot was the second ball for the fifth frame strike. Ron missed the spare. Add nine to his sixth and seventh frame scores. **Eighth frame**: Ron fouled on his first shot, so the scorer places an F on the sheet. Ron threw a nice pocket ball on his second shot and knocked down all 10 pins. Because it was the second

shot, and not the first, it is recorded as a spare. **Ninth frame**: Ron threw a strike in the frame, to add 10 pins to the eighth-frame spare total. **10th frame**: Ron could throw three strikes in this frame, but he pulled the shot to the left and knocked down only six pins. If he gets the spare, he would get a third shot to complete the game. If he misses the four pins in the spare shot, he does not get a third ball. Ron picked up the spare, and got eight pins on his third shot to finish the game with a 181 total.

Keeping score in bowling looks a lot more difficult than it really is. Usually, as soon as new bowlers figure out that a spare counts 10 pins plus whatever the bowler gets on the next ball, and a strike counts 10 pins plus whatever the bowler gets on the next two balls, keeping score is easy. If you never learn how to keep score you can get by today because there

Fast Facts

Earl Anthony, six-time Professional Bowler of the Year, was the first to earn $100,000 in a single season ($107,585 in 1975) and the first to earn more than $1 million in a career. He recorded 41 PBA championships. He was born April 27, 1938.

FIGURING AVERAGES

Bowling averages are determined by dividing the number of games bowled by the total of those games. For example, if you bowl three games and the total of those games is 480 your average is 480 divided by 3, which is an even 160. Your average is an important number because it is used to determine the handicap you will receive in league and tournament handicap competition.

Example: Bowler completes 24 games. Total score of the 24 games is 3,775 pins. To get the bowler's average divide 3,775 by 24. In this case the bowler's average is 157. Fractions (see the .29 below) are dropped in figuring averages.

$$\frac{\text{Average}}{\text{Total of game scores}} \quad \text{Number of games}$$

$$24\ \overline{)\ 3{,}775}\quad 157.29$$

```
              157.29
      ┌─────────────
24    │ 3,775
        24
        ───
        137
        120
        ───
        175
        168
        ───
         70
         68
```

KNOW THE PINS

Each pin in the rack of 10 is numbered. Knowing the numbers of each pin is a good idea because so many bowlers refer to them by number. For example, you try to put your ball in the 1-3 or 1-2 pocket to get a strike. You always try to avoid the big 7-10 split, so you do not want to hit the head pin (1-pin) too solid. A baby split could be either the 3-10 leave or the 2-7 leave. If you hit the pocket and leave the 5-pin, that usually means your ball did not carry well. A solid hit in the pocket that leaves a 7, 8, 9 or 10 pin is called a tap. A solid hit in the pocket that leaves a 7-9 or 8-10 is called a strike tap.

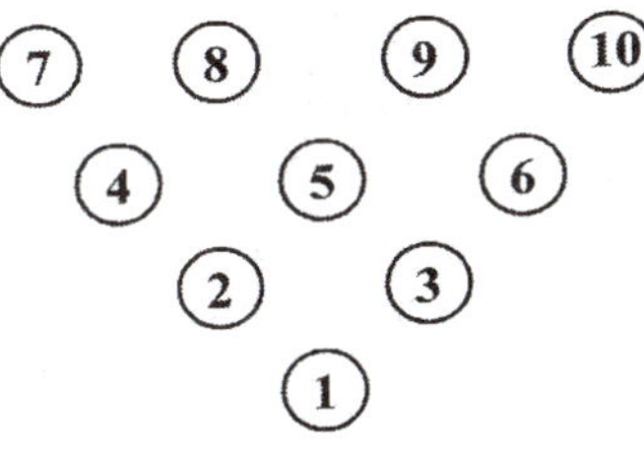

71

FIGURING HANDICAPS

Bowling handicaps are figured in a variety of ways, but the basis for all handicaps is a bowler's average. Handicaps help make competition more even between high average bowlers and lower average bowlers as lower average bowlers are given extra pins (a handicap) to make up some of the difference between the two bowlers. Common handicaps range from 70 to 90 percent of the difference between a bowler's average and selected arbitrary averages that usually range from 180 to 240.

One of the most common handicaps is 90 percent of the difference between a bowler's average and an arbitrary average of 210. Here is how that is figured: Subtract the bowler's average from 210. If the bowler's average was 155, you take 155 from 210. That equals 55. To get 90 percent of 55 simply multiply 55 by point-nine. (If the handicap is to be 70 or 80 percent you would multiply by point-seven or point-eight.) In this case the bowler's handicap is 49. Fractions are dropped in figuring handicaps.

Here is an example of how to figure a handicap for a bowler with a 160 average in a league where the handicap is 90 percent of the difference between 210 and the bowler's average:

STEP ONE	**STEP TWO**
210 (Selected Handicap Basis)	Multiply difference (50) by
-160 (Bowler's Average)	the percentage: 50 X .9 = 45
50 (Difference in average and handicap score.)	Handicap is 45 pins per game

Note to lower average bowlers: Don't let the big average bowlers razz you about giving them too many pins in handicap matches. In all handicap cases except when the handicap is 100 percent, the higher average bowler has the advantage. In a 90 percent handicap league the high average bowler has a 10 percent advantage, in an 80 percent handicap league the higher average bowler has a 20 percent advantage. In other words, if both bowlers hit their averages, the higher average bowler will win every time.

*See the 90 and 80 percent handicap charts in the back of *Bowler's Handbook* for easy figuring.

COURTESY IN BOWLING

Bowling courtesy is not unlike the Golden Rule of "do unto others as you would have them do unto you." The practice of manners simply allows bowling to be more enjoyable for everyone, including spectators. Good manners are appropriate in all situations, but in bowling there are a few special courtesy rules. Here, in no order of importance, are a few of them:

❖ Be ready to bowl when it is your turn. If you have to go to the rest room, snack bar, lockers or some other place during bowling, do it when you are least likely to hold up the game.

❖ Yield to the bowler on your left or right if they are ready to bowl ahead of you. Yielding means give them the go-ahead and stay out of their line of sight. A bowler shooting a spare has the right of way over a bowler shooting for a strike. If, however, you see a bowler shooting to continue a string of strikes or a 300 game, get out of the way. Be aware of your surroundings on the lane.

❖ Show up. If you agree to bowl on a team for a season, you are expected to be at the lanes at least 15 minutes (half hour is better) before the scheduled time to bowl. If you have to miss a scheduled match, call

your captain as soon as possible and let that person know you will not be there. The captain can make arrangements for a substitute. Individual bowlers are usually responsible for payment each night the team is scheduled to bowl. Various payment arrangements are made in various leagues, but the bottom line is if you agree to bowl, you are responsible to be there and pay for bowling.

❖ Don't linger on the approach or at the foul line. When it is your turn to bowl, take a reasonable amount of time to set up and make your delivery. After you release the ball and you have seen your shot, return to the back of the approach.

❖   Stay in your area on the approach after you deliver the ball. Bowlers who wander to the adjoining approaches risk injury and disrupting other bowlers.

❖   Keep loud noise to a minimum. It is great to cheer for your teammates, but don't do it in such a way that it might distract other bowlers.

❖   Don't loft or drop the bowling ball during your release in a way that will damage the lanes.

❖   Don't give bowling advice unless you are asked for it.

❖   Bragging in any sport or activity is a bad idea.

❖   Be a good sport. Everyone has bad nights, missed spares and eight- and ninepin counts on balls buried in the pocket. Don't rant and rave, and do not slam the equipment. Cry babies aren't popular anywhere.

❖   Watch your language. Bad language is not welcome anyplace, and it is especially not needed in areas where there may be children.

❖   Many bowlers carry two or three balls or more. Leave your main ball on the ball return, and keep the others in a handy place not on the seats to allow room for each bowler to have a ball on the return and a place to sit.

❖   Don't leave your towel in a seat or on the bowling balls in the ball rack. Other bowlers should not have to move your towel to sit down or pickup a ball.

❖   Don't use someone else's equipment without permission. Bowlers are touchy (and sometimes superstitious) about their equipment.

❖   Learn and follow the bowling center rules. Most centers today do not allow smoking (usually a state or local law), do not allow drinks in the immediate bowling area, and require bowlers to wear bowling shoes.

❖   Finally, a word about hygiene: If you have to rush to the lanes after a long day at work, you are probably not as "fresh" as you might be. Try to schedule your time so you get a chance to shower, brush your teeth and put on some clean clothing before going bowling. You'll feel better, and so will your teammates.

BOWLING RULES

Here is an overview of the rules most frequently used in bowling. Complete rule books, issued by the United States Bowling Congress, are available free at most bowling centers.

Game - Definition

Rule 2a. A game of American tenpins consists of 10 frames. A player delivers two balls in each of the first nine frames unless a strike is scored. In the 10th frame, a player delivers three balls if a strike or spare is scored. Every frame must be completed by each player bowling in regular order.

Legal Delivery

Rule 4a. A delivery is made when the ball leaves the player's possession and crosses the foul line into playing territory. Every delivery counts unless a dead ball is declared. A delivery must be made entirely by manual means. No device may be incorporated in or affixed to the ball that detaches on delivery or is a moving part during delivery except as provided in Rules 4b and c (rules for amputees).

Foul Detection

Rule 5c. A USBC approved automatic foul detecting device must be used if available. When not available, a foul judge must be stationed in position to have an unobstructed view of the foul line.   ....failure to provide for the calling of fouls as specified shall disqualify scores bowled for USBC high score award consideration.

Illegal Pinfall

Rule 6b. When any of the following occur the delivery counts but the resulting pinfall does not:

1. A ball leaves the lane before reaching the pins.

2. A ball rebounds from the rear cushion.

3. A pin rebounds after coming in contact with the body, arms or legs of a human pinsetter.

4. A pin is touched by mechanical pin-setting equipment.

5. Any pin knocked down when dead wood is being removed.

6. Any pin knocked down by a human pinsetter.

7. The player commits a foul.

8. A delivery is made with dead wood on the lane or in the gutter and the ball contacts such dead wood before leaving the lane surface.

If illegal pin fall occurs and the player is entitled to additional deliveries in the frame, the pin(s) illegally knocked down must be re-spotted where they originally stood before delivery of the ball.

Pins - Improperly Set

Rule 7a. It is each player's responsibility to determine if a setup is correct. The player shall insist that any pin(s) incorrectly set be re-spotted before delivering the ball, otherwise the setup is deemed to be acceptable.

Dead Ball

Rule 8. When a dead ball is called, the delivery does not count and the correct pins must be re-spotted. The player is allowed to re-bowl that delivery.

A ball shall be declared dead if any of the following occur:

a. After a delivery, attention is immediately called to the fact that one or more pins were missing from the setup.

b. A human pinsetter interferes with any standing pin before the ball reaches the pins.

c. A human pinsetter removes or interferes with any downed pin before it stops rolling.

d. A player bowls on the wrong lane or out of turn. Or one player from each team on the pair of lanes bowls on the wrong lane.

e. A player is interfered with by the pinsetter, another player, spectator, or moving object as the ball is being delivered and before delivery is completed. In such case, the player has the option to accept the resulting pinfall or have a dead ball called.

f. Any pin is moved or knocked down as a player delivers the ball but before the ball reaches the pins.

g. A delivered ball comes in contact with a foreign obstacle.

Forfeit - Delay of Game

Rule 11. No unreasonable delay in the progress of any game is permitted. If a player or team in a league or tournament refuses to proceed with a game after being directed to do so by a league or tournament official, the game or series shall be declared forfeited.

Bowling Ball - Altering Surface

Rule 18. Altering the surface of a bowling ball by the use of abrasives while bowling in USBC competition is prohibited. All bowling balls so altered must be removed from the competition.

The use of approved cleaning agents such as isopropyl (rubbing) alcohol and polishing machines is permissible.

BOWLING EQUIPMENT

Most bowlers who bowl regularly own equipment even though bowling centers rent bowling shoes and allow free use of lane balls. Some bowlers carry the complete list of equipment, including a variety of bowling balls to match particular lane conditions, while some bowlers carry only a ball and a pair of bowling shoes in a bowling bag. Bowling equipment can be purchased in a variety of places, including the bowling center pro shop, sporting goods stores, on-line and at a few department stores.

Here is a list of the equipment bowlers can use:

❖**Bowling shoes** come in a variety of styles, but have one thing in common: they are made to allow the bowler to slide easily on one foot and stop with the other foot. The sliding shoe (left for right handed bowlers and right for lefties) usually has a sole of leather or man-made material that allows sliding, while the sole on the other shoe is usually made of rubber or a material to help the bowler stop the slide. Get a pair of shoes that fit comfortably. Prices vary from $20 to more than $100 in bowling center pro shops, on-line distributors, sporting goods stores and department stores. *Care*: Wipe off the shoes with a damp cloth, and clean the rubber areas – heels and non-sliding side – with a cloth dipped in rubbing  alcohol. Use a soft wire brush to remove tough substances from the sliding surface. To enhance sliding use a powder made to put on the bottom of the shoe. Be careful not to use too much, and test the shoes by sliding on the approach before you actually bowl. Don't use a shoe polish because it can get on the approach.

❖If you happen to walk any place in the bowling center away from the immediate bowling area, you should have a pair of **shoe covers** to protect you from getting something on the bottom of your bowling shoes. Just a spot of liquid or a piece of candy on the bottom of your sliding shoe can lead to an accident you do not need.

❖Put an extra pair of **shoestrings** in your bowling bag just in case.

❖Carry a **soft wire brush** for roughing and cleaning the sliding surface.

❖**Bowling balls** come in hundreds of colors made in a variety of materials that do and do not promote hook action. Bowling beginners should wait until they have a good idea of their individual style and needs before purchasing a ball, and when they are ready they should seek advice from an area bowling coach, a pro-shop operator, or a good, knowledgable bowler they know and trust.

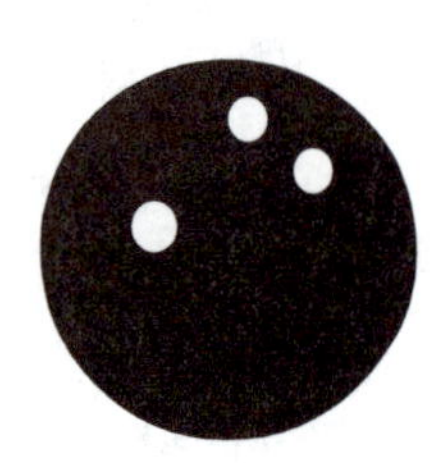

Balls are made in weights from 8 to 16 pounds. Most top male bowlers use 15-pound balls, while female bowlers tend to use 12- to 14-pound balls. Many international bowlers use 12-pound balls very successfully. Technically, a 15-pound ball thrown two miles per hour faster than a 16-pound ball has more hitting power.

The bottom line in determining what weight ball to use is it should match the bowler's ability to use it without strain. Balls can be drilled for four finger holes and a thumb hole. The standard is two finger holes and a thumb hole. Prices for new balls range from $25 to more than

BALL HOOKING CHART

Each of the basic four cover stocks can be polished or sanded to create less or more hooking ability. Hooking potential also is very dependant on the bowler's ability, ball speed and lane conditions.

LEAST

PLASTIC
Polished 0-3 boards
Sanded 1-5 boards

URETHANE
Polished 3-8 boards
Sanded 5-10 boards

REACTIVE RESIN
Polished 3-12 boards
Sanded 5-15 boards

STRONGEST

PARTICLE
Polished 5-15 boards
Sanded 8-20 boards

$200, with most balls being sold in the range of $60 to $130. Basically, balls are manufactured today with a surface of four materials: plastic, urethane, reactive resin and particle. In addition to the basic material balls, many older rubber bowling balls are still around. Generally, plastic, polished urethane and rubber have the least hook potential. Sanded urethane balls have the next highest hook potential. Those balls have a rating of from five to 10 boards (*being able to hook across that many boards on a lane*). A sanded reactive resin ball has a hook potential of five to 15 boards. Sanded particle balls, with a rating of eight to 20 boards, have the greatest hook potential. Bowlers should note, however, that hook potential and curve potential is dependant on lane conditions and very dependant on the bowler's ability.

So, again, before beginning bowlers plunk down cash for a bowling ball, they should have a good idea of what to expect from a ball, they should match their style with a particular ball, and they should seek advice from knowledgeable bowlers, bowling coaches and/or pro shop operators. Many pro shops carry used balls that can be drilled to match the bowler.

Care: Most ball manufacturers recommend cleaning the bowling ball immediately after bowling. Of course, they recommend using their ball-cleaning products to remove lane dirt and oil. Many bowlers use inexpensive isopropyl alcohol, which is also permitted for use during bowling. Most bowlers wipe the ball with a soft towel each frame as a part of a pre-shot routine. Do not store bowling balls where they will be subject to extreme temperatures. *Quick Fact: The first bowling balls in the United States were made of a very hard wood called lignum vitae. A few Lignum vitae trees still grow in the Florida Keys.*

❖**Finger Inserts** of rubber are fairly standard in newly drilled balls. The inserts give the bowler a little better finger grip and subsequent better lift on the ball. They come in all sizes and in a variety of colors. Pro shops, sporting goods stores and bowling equipment suppliers on the Internet sell finger inserts. *Care*: When finger inserts wear out, simply replace them.

❖**Insert Tapes** come in two main forms, those for better grip and those to promote sliding in tight thumb holes. Your fingers and thumbs have a tendency to shrink and swell, so that is best taken care of by inserting the appropriate tapes in the bowling ball finger and thumb holes. *Care*: Keep your finger holes and thumb holes clean. There are several products, including inexpensive lighter fluid, to remove tape residue.

❖**<u>Bowling bags/carriers</u>** are made to carry from one to eight bowling balls. New bowlers should get a bag large enough to carry one or two balls, shoes, towel, paper and pen for notes, and various rosins. The prices for new bags range from $20 up. Many bowling ball carriers are equipped with wheels. If you intend to carry more than one bowling ball, we recommend getting wheeled bags. *Care*: Dust the carrier off regularly, and at least once a year take everything out of it and clean it out. Store your carrier and equipment in a dry place

❖**<u>Towels</u>** are important for ball care and hand care. Most bowlers carry a soft hand-towel to wipe off their hands and the ball each frame. *Care*: It is a good idea to regularly wash the towel because if you use it to wipe your hands and the ball each frame, it gets plenty of use and picks up a lot of lane oil and dirt.

❖**<u>Chalks, rosins and baby powder</u>** are used for a variety of purposes, including drying hands, giving a bowler better grip on the bowling ball, and in the case of baby powder eliminating sticking in tight thumb holes. Some people use **<u>chap stick</u>** for the same purpose. *Care*: It is best to keep these products in sealed bags to prevent spilling. Be careful that you do not get any of these products, especially powder, on the approach.

❖**<u>Wrist and hand supports</u>** are used by many bowlers, including a number of professionals, to insure more consistent deliveries and provide support for people with weaker, injured or arthritic hands and wrists. These items can be found in most pro shops, sporting goods stores, pharmacies, department/variety stores and on the Internet.

❖**<u>Carpal tunnel and tennis elbow supports</u>** can be worn just below the elbow on your bowling arm to give some relief from those problems.

❖Miscellaneous items might include a **<u>band-aid</u>** or two in case of a blister or scratch, **<u>pencil and paper</u>** to keep notes, a **<u>personal score sheet</u>**, and **<u>small calculator</u>** for quick totals and averages.

DRESS IN BOWLING

One of the neat things about bowling is that except for shoes, you can wear just about anything you want to bowl. The only universal requirement in bowling is that you should wear bowling shoes that allow you to slide on the approach properly when delivering the ball. Avoid clothing that could get in the way of your delivery, or that is too tight to restrict your movement. *Note: If you are one of the lucky bowlers given a team shirt from a sponsor, it is courtesy to keep it clean and wear it when your team competes.*

FAST FACTS --- Some Home Towns

Patrick Allen, Terrytown, N.Y.

Ritchie Allen, Columbia, S.C.

Brad Angelo, Lockport, N.Y.

Diandra Asbaty, Chicago, Ill.

Parker Bohn III, Jackson, N.J.

Neil Burton, St. Charles, Mo.

Andrew Cain, Chandler, Ariz.

Dave Callery, Cincinnati, Ohio

Frank Carr, Fort Wayne, Ind.

Don Carter, Miami, Fla.

Paul Colwell, Tucson, Ariz.

Jason Couch, Clermont, Fla.

Pete Couture, Titusville, Fla.

Tim Criss, Bel Air, Md.

Dave Davis, West Palm Beach, Fla.

Gary Dickinson, Edmond, Okla.

Donald Dobs, Milwaukee, Wisc.

Bill Doehrmann, Fort Wayne, Ind.

Kevin Dornberger, Sioux Falls, S.D.

Anne Marie Duggan, Edmond, Okla.

Mike Durbin, Boulder City, Nev.

Dale Eagle, Lewisville, Texas

John Eiss, Brooklyn Park, Minn.

Frank Ellenburg, Chandler, Ariz.

Steve Fehr, Cincinnati, Ohio

John Gaines, Davidsonville, Md.

Bob Glass, Lawrence, Kans.

Greg Griffo, Syracuse, N.Y.

Bob Hanson, Richfield, Minn.

Patrick Healey Jr., Dallas, Tx.

Steve Hoskins, Tarpon Springs, Fla.

Steve Jaros, Yorkville, Ill.

Liz Johnson, Tonawanda, N.Y.

Tommy Jones, Simsonville, S.C.

Alisia Kellow, Louisville, Ky.

Debbie Kuhn, Baltimore, Md.

Bob Larson, Knosha, Wisc.

Hank Marino, Milwaukee, Wis.

Bobby Meadows, Arlington, Tx.

Tennelle Milligan, Costa Mesa, Cal.

Stefanie National, Miami, Fla.

Glen Olson, Boulder City, Nev.

George Pappas, Charlotte, N.C.

Randy Pedersen, Hollywood, Fla.

Jim Peneak, Cleveland, Ohio

Shannon Pluhowsky, Chalmette, La

Barb Ripley, Bradenton, Fla.

Mike Samardzija, Pontiac, Mich.

Derek Sapp, Keokuk, Iowa

Don Scudder, Cincinnati, Ohio

Mike Scroggins, Amarillo, Tx.

Aleta Sill, Dearborn, Mich.

Gene Stus, Allen Park, Mich.

Mike Surina, Spokane, Wash.

Gordon Vadakin, Wichita, Kan.

Brian Voss, Atlanta, Ga.

Linda Wallace, Tucson, Ariz.

Sharon Wanczyk, Crofton, Md.

Dick Weber, St. Louis, Mo.

Pete Weber, St. Ann, Mo.

John Wilcox, Lewisburg, Pa.

Bill Young, Homer, N.Y.

BOWLING AWARDS

The United States Bowling Congress offers a number of awards to USBC members bowling in USBC sanctioned leagues. Members are eligible for one award during a fiscal year in these categories:

Individual Single Game:
a. A 300 game.
b. A 299 game.
c. A 298 game.
d. 250 to 297 with a 170 average or below.
e. 200 to 249 with a 160 average or below.
f. 180 to 199 with a 140 average or below.
g. 160 to 179 with a 120 average or below.
h. 140 to 159 with a 100 average or below.
i. 120 to 139 with a 90 average or below.
j. 100 to 119 with a 70 average or below.
k. 80 to 99 with a 50 average or below.
l. Eleven (11) strikes in a row when the score is 297 or less.
m. 100 pins over game average.
n. 75 pins over game average.

Individual Series (3 games):
a. 900 series.
b. 800 to 899 series.
c. 700 to 799 with a 210 average or less.
d. 600 to 699 with a 175 average or less.
e. 500 to 599 with a 140 average or less.
f. 400 to 499 with a 115 average or less.
g. 300 to 399 with a 90 average or less.
h. 200 to 299 with a 50 average or less.
i. 140 pins over series average.

Team Awards:
Men's Teams —

5-player:	1,325 game.	3,700 series.
4-player	1,050 game.	2,900 series.
3-player	825 game	2,250 series.
2-player	550 game	1,550 series.

Mixed Teams –

5-player:	1,250 game.	3,600 series.
4-player	1,000 game.	2,800 series.
3-player	750 game	2,200 series.
2-player	525 game	1,500 series.

Women's Teams –

5-player:	1,175 game.	3,425 series.
4-player	950 game.	2,750 series.
3-player	725 game	2,075 series.
2-player	500 game	1,350 series.

Youth Teams –

(To determine age group, use the age of the oldest bowler.)

	2-Player		3-Player		4-Player		5-Player	
Age Group	Game	Series	Game	Series	Game	Series	Game	Series
8 and under	140	420	210	630	280	840	350	1050
9 -11	200	600	300	900	400	1200	500	1500
12 -14	260	780	390	1170	520	1560	650	1950
15 -18	350	1050	525	1575	700	2100	875	2625
19 - 22	420	1260	630	1890	840	2520	1050	3150

Special Achievement Awards for all USBC bowlers

1. Conversion of the 7-10 split.

2. Conversion of the 4-6-7-10 split.

3. All spares in a game.

4. Dutch 200 game —A game in which strikes and spares are regiestered in alternating frames with a game total score of 200.

5. Triplicate series — Three consecutive games of the same score in a series.

Average & League Awards

The USBC also issues awards for the male, female, youth male and female having the highest USBC average in the nation based on 66 or more games bowled as a USBC member in a USBC sanctioned league.

The USBC also issues awards for the highest series bowled nationally by a male, female, youth male and female.

Leagues also offer additional awards. See your league officials to get a list of those awards.

HALL OF FAME BOWLERS

U.S. BOWLING CONGRESS HALL OF FAME MEMBERS
(Performance Section) *(The year listed is when the bowler was inducted)*

(A) Glenn Allison (1979).   Earl Anthony (1986). Barry Asher (1998). Harold Asplund (1978). Mike Aulby (2001).

(B) Gordy Baer (1987). Bill Beach (1991). Frank Benkovic (1958). Mike Berlin (1994). George Billick (1982). Jimmy Blouin (1953). Ray Bluth (1973). Joe Bodis (1941). Buddy Bomar (1966). Gary Bower (2001). Allie Brandt (1960). Eddie Brosius (1976). Fred Bujack (1967). Bill Bunetta (1968). Nelson Burton Sr. (1964). Nelson Burton Jr. (1981).

(C) Lou Campi (1968). Adolph Carlson (1941). Don Carter (1970). Frank Caruana (1977). Marty Cassio (1972). Graz Castellano (1976). Bob Chamberlain (2005). Frank Clause (1980). Alfred Cohn (1985). Paul Colwell (1999). Pete Couture (2004). John Crimmins (1962).

(D) Dave Davis (1990). Charlie Daw (1941). Ned Day (1952). Gary Dickinson (1992). Norm Duke (2002).

(E) Sarge Easter (1963). Don Ellis (1981).

(F) Joe Falcaro (1975). Lindy Faragalli (1968). Buzz Fazio (1963). Steve Fehr (1993).

(G) Russ Geronde (1968). Therm Gibson (1965). Jim Godman (1987). Bob Goike (1996). Billy Golembiewski (1979). Greg Griffo (1995). John Guenther (1988).

(H) Bob Hanson (2004). Billy Hardwick (1985). Bob Hart (1994). Tom Hennessey (1976). Dick Hoover (1974). Bud Horn (1992). George Howard (1986).

(J) Eddie Jackson (1988). Lowell Jackson (2003). Mark Jensen (2002). Don Johnson (1982). Earl Johnson (1987). Joe Joseph (1969). Lee Jouglard (1979).

(K) Frank Kartheiser (1967). Ed Kawolics (1966). Joe Kissoff (1976). John Klares (1982). John Koster (1941). Eddie Krems (1973). Joe Kristof (1968). Paul Krumske (1968).

(L) Herb Lange (1941). Hank Lauman (1976). Mark Lewis (2004). Bill Lillard (1972). Tony Lindemann (1979). Mort Lindsey (1941). Harry Lippe (1989). Ed Lubanski (1971). Vince Lucci Sr. (1978).

(M) Hank Marino (1941). John Martino (1969). Andy Marzich (1993). Mike McGrath (1993). Junie McMahon (1955). Darold Meisel (1998).

Walter "Skang" Mercurio (1967). Norm Meyers (1984).
(N) Steve Nagy (1963). Joe Norris (1954).
(O) Charles O'Donnell (1968).
(P) George Pappas (1989). Claude "Pat" Patterson (1974). John "Junior" Powell (2000).
(R) Dick Ritger (1984). Andy Rogoznica (1993).
(S) Carmen Salvino (1979). Tod Savoy (2005). Les Schissler (1991). Ernie Schlegel (1997). Jim Schroeder (1990). Conrad "Connie" Schwoegler (1968). Don Scudder (1999). Teata Semiz (1991). Louis Sielaff (1968). Joe Sinke (1977). Billy Sixty (1961). Harry Smith (1978). Jimmy Smith (1941). Dave Soutar (1985). Tony Sparando (1968). Bill Spigner (2001). Barney Spinella (1968). Harry Steers (1941). Jim Stefanich (1983). Otto Stein Jr. (1971). Bud Stoudt (1991). Bob Strampe (1977).
(T) Frank "Sykes" Thoma (1971). Rod Toft (1991). Mike Totsky (1996). Pete Tountas (1989). Bill Tucker (1988). Tommy Tuttle (1995).
(V) Andy Varipapa (1975).
(W) Walter Ward (1959). Dick Weber (1970). Peter Weber (2002). Billy Welu (1975). John Wilcox (1999). Walter Ray Williams (2005). Joe Wilman (1951). Phil Wolf (1961). Rich Wonders (1990).
(Z) Wayne Zahn (1980). Les Zikes (1983). Gil Zunker (1941)

WIBC HALL OF FAME (Performance Section)

(Year listed is when the bowler was inducted.)

(A) Joy Abel (1984). Donna Adamek (1996). Patty Ann (1995).
(B) Mae Bolt (1978). Gloria Bouvia (1987). Loa Boxberger (1984). Catherine Burling (1958). Nina Burns (1977).
(C) Anita Cantaline (1979). LaVerne Carter (1977). Paula Carter (1994). Doris Coburn (1976). Cindy Coburn-Carroll (1998). Pat Costello (1986). Patty Costello (1989).
(D) Cheryl Daniels (2002). Pat Dryer (1978). Helen Duval (1970).
(F) Catherine Fellmeth (1970). Cora Fiebig (2004). Dorothy Fothergill (1980). Deane Fritz (1966).Louise Fulton (2001).
(G) Shirley Garms (1971). Nikki Gianulias (1997). Olga Gloor (1976). Ashie Gonzalez (1998). Linda Graham (1992). Mary Lou Graham (1989). Goldie Greenwald (1953). Vesma Grinfelds (1991).
(H) Janet Harman (1985). Stella Hartrick (1972). Grayce Hatch (1953). Jean Havlish (1987). Martha Hoffman (1979). Joan Holm (1974). Birdie Humphreys (1979).

(I) Millie Martorella Ignizio (1975).

(J) D.D. Jacobson (1981). Emma Jaeger (1953). Tish Johnson (2002).

(K) Annese Kelly (1985). Linda Kelly (2003). Doris Knechtges (1983). Betty Kuczynski (1981).

(L) Marion Ladewig (1964).

(M) Merle Matthews (1974). Floretta McCutcheon (1956). Marge Merrick (1980). Val Mikiel (1979). Dana Miller-Mackey (2000). Carol Miller (1997). Dorothy Miller (1954). Betty Mivelaz (1991). Mary Mohacsi (1994). Betty Morris (1983).

(N) Jeanne Naccarato (1999). Lorrie Koch Nichols (1989). Carol Norman (2001). Edie Jo Norman (1993). Virginia Norton (1988). Phyllis Notaro (1979).

(O) Bev Ortner (1972).

(P) Connie Powers (1973).

(R) Susie Reichley (2000). Robbie Rickard (1994). Leona Robinson (1969). Robin Romeo (1995). Anita Rump (1962). Addie Ruschmeyer (1961). Esther Ryan (1963).

(S) Ethel Sablatnik (1979). Lucy Sandelin (1999). Myrtle Schulte (1965). Helen Shablis (1977). Aleta Sill (1996). Violet "Billy" Simon (1960). DTess Small (1971). Judy Soutar (1976). Louise Stockdale (1953).

(T) Elvira Toepfer (1976). Sally Twyford (1964).

(W) Lisa Wagner (2000). Marie Warmbier (1953). Sylvia Wene-Martin (1966). Dorothy Wilkinson (1990). Cecelia Winandy (1975).

(Z) Donna Zimmerman (1982).

Fast Facts

Walter Ray Williams Jr., Ocala, Fla., 2005 inductee in the USBC Bowlers Hall of Fame, is a six-time world horseshoe pitching champion, has a three handicap in golf, and holds a Bachelor of Science degree in physics from Cal-Poly University, Pomona, Calif. Williams has won 41 career Professional Bowler's Association tour championships, equaled only by Hall of Fame bowler Earl Anthony. Williams was PBA Player of the Year in 1986, 1993, 1996, 1997, 1998 and 2003. The 46-year-old Williams has won $3.5 million on the PBA Tour while bowling nearly 20,000 games in more than 600 tour events. In 1993 Williams became the first on the tour to average more than 220 when he averaged 222.98.

BOWLING WRITERS ASSOCIATION OF AMERICA BOWLERS OF THE YEAR

Female Bowlers of the Year --

2004 - Shannon Pluhowsky, Pheonix. 2003 - Carolyn Dorin-Ballard, Dallas. 2002- Leanne Barrette, Pleasanton, Calif. 2001 - Carolyn Dorin-Ballard, Dallas. 2000 - Wendy Macpherson, Henderson, Nev. 1999 - Wendy Macpherson, Henderson, Nev. 1998 - Carol Gianotti-Block, Australia. 1997 - Wendy Macpherson, Henderson, Nev. 1996 - Wendy Macpherson, Henderson, Nev. 1995 - Tish Johnson, Northridge, Calif. 1994 - Anne Marie Duggan, Edmond, Okla. 1993 - Lisa Wagner, Palmetto, Fla. 1992 - Tish Johnson, Panorama, Calif. 1991 - Leanne Barrette, Yukon, Okla. 1990 - Tish Johnson, Panarama, Calif. 1989 - Robin Romeo, Newhall, Calif. 1988 - Lisa Wagner, Palmetto, Fla. 1987 - Betty Morris, Stockton, Calif. 1986 - Lisa Wagner, Palmetto, Fla. 1985 - Aleta Sill, Dearborn, Mich. 1984 - Aleta Sill, Dearborn, Mich. 1983 - Lisa Wagner, Palmetto, Fla. 1982 - Nikki Gianulias, Vallejo, Calif. 1981 - Donna Adamek, Apple Valley, Calif. 1982 - Donna Adamek, Apple Valley, Calif. 1981 - Donna Adamek, Apple Valley, Calif. 1980- Donna Adamek, Apple Valley, Calif. 1979 - Donna Adamek, Apple Valley, Calif. 1978 - Donna Adamek, Apple Valley, Calif. 1976 - Patty Costello, Scranton, Pa. 1975 - Judy Soutar, Leawood, Kans. 1974 - Betty Morris, Stockton, Calif. 1973 - Judy Soutar, Leawood, Kans. 1972 - Patty Costello, Scranton, Pa. 1971 - Paula Carter, Miami, Fla. 1970 - Mary Baker Harris, Cent. Islip, N.Y. 1969 - Dorothy Fothergill, Ossippee, N.H. 1968 - Dorothy Fothergill, Ossippee, N.H. 1967 - Mildred Ignizio, Rochester, N.Y. 1966 - Joy Abel, Lansing, Mich. 1965 - Betty Kuczynski, Chicago. 1964 - LaVerne Carter, Las Vagas. 1963 - Marion Ladewig, Grand Rapids, Mich. 1962 - Shirley Garms, Island Lake, Ill. 1961 - Shirley Garms, Island Lake, Ill. 1960 - Sylvia Martin, Philadelphia. 1959 - Marion Ladewig, Grand Rapids, Mich. 1958 - Marion Ladewig, Grand Rapids, Mich. 1957 - Marion Ladewig, Grand Rapids, Mich. 1956 - Anita Cantaline, Detroit. 1955 - Sylvia Martin, Philadelphia. 1954 - Marion Ladewig, Grand Rapids, Mich. 1953 - Marion Ladewig, Grand Rapids, Mich. 1952 - Marion Ladewig, Grand Rapids, Mich. 1951 - Marion Ladewig, Grand Rapids, Mich. 1950 - Marion Ladewig, Grand Rapids, Mich. 1949 - Val Mikel, Detroit. 1948 - Val Mikel, Detroit.

Male Bowlers of the Year --

2004 - Walter Ray Williams Jr., Ocala, Fla. 2003 - Walter Ray Williams Jr., Ocala, Fla. 2002 - Walter Ray Williams Jr., Ocala, Fla. 2001 - Parker Bohn III, Jackson, N.J. 2000 - Norm Duke, Clermont, Fla. 1999 - Parker Bohn III, Jackson, N.J. 1998 - Walter Ray Williams Jr., Ocala, Fla. 1997 - Walter Ray Williams Jr., Ocala, Fla. 1996 - Walter Ray Williams Jr., Ocala, Fla. 1995 - Mike Aulby, Indianapolis. 1994 - Norm Duke, Edmond, Okla. 1993 - Walter Ray Williams Jr., Stockton, Calif. 1992 - Marc McDowell, Madison, Wisc. 1991 - David Ozio, Vido, Texas. 1990 - Amleto Monacelli, Venezuela. 1989 - Mike Aulby, Indianapolis. 1988 - Brian Voss, Tacoma, Wash. 1987 - Marshall Holman, Medford, Ore. 1986 - Walter Ray Williams Jr., Stockton, Calif. 1985 - Mike Aulby, Indianapolis. 1984 - Mark Roth, Spring Lake Hts., N.J. 1983 - Earl Anthony, Dublin Calif. 1982 - Earl Anthony, Dublin Calif. 1981 - Earl Anthony, Dublin Calif. 1980 - Wayne Webb, Reheboth, Mass. 1979 - Mark Roth, N. Arlington, N.J. 1978 - Mark Roth, N. Arlington, N.J. 1977 - Mark Roth, N. Arlington, N.J. 1976 - Earl Anthony, Dublin Calif. 1975 - Earl Anthony, Dublin Calif. 1974 - Earl Anthony, Dublin Calif. 1973 - Don McCune, Munster, Ind. 1972 - Don Johnson, Akron, Ohio. 1971 - Don Johnson, Akron, Ohio. 1970 - Nelson Burton Jr., St. Louis. 1969 - Billy Hardwick, Louisville, Ky. 1968 - Jim Stefanich, Joliet, Ill. 1967 - Dave Davis, Pheonix. 1966 - Wayne Zahn, Atlanta. 1965 - Dick Weber, St. Louis. 1964 - Billy Hardwick, San Mateo, Calif. 1963 - Dick Weber, St. Louis. 1962 - Don Carter, St. Louis. 1961 - Dick Weber, St. Louis. 1960 - Don Carter, St. Louis. 1959 - Ed Lubanski, Detroit. 1958 - Don Carter, St. Louis. 1957 - Don Carter, St. Louis. 1956 - Bill Lillard, Chicago. 1955 - Steve Nagy, Detroit. 1954 - Don Carter, St. Louis. 1953 - Don Carter, St. Louis. 1952 - Steve Nagy, Cleveland. 1951 Lee Jouglard, Detroit. 1950 - Junie McMahon, Fair Lawn, N.J. 1949 - Connie Schwoegler, Madison, Wis. 1948 - Andy Varipapa, Brooklyn, N.Y. 1947 - Buddy Bomar, Chicago. 1944 - Ned Day, Milwaukee. 1943 - Ned Day, Milwaukee. 1942 - Johnny Crimmins, Detroit.

Senior Bowlers of the Year --

2004 - Robert Glass, Shirley Levens. 2003 - Robert Glass, Shirley Levens. 2002- Robert Glass, Shirley Levens. 2001 - Robert Glass, Frank Deken. 2000 - Robert Glass, Linda Kelly. 1999 - Dale Eagle. 1998 - Pete Couture. 1997 - Gary Dickinson. 1996 - Earl Anthony. 1995 - Tommy Evans. 1994 - John Handegard. 1993 - Gary Dickinson.

NATIONAL BOWLING RECORDS
League Individual Averages
(Minimum of 66 games)

Men

261.7   Jeff Carter, Springfield, Ill. 2000-2001

256.8   Mike Scroggins, Amarillo, Tex. 1999-2000

251.2   Chris Lucas, Bonesteel, SD. 2003-2004

251.2   William Young, Homer, N.Y. 2004-2005

Women

244   Liz Johnson, Buffalo, N.Y. 2005-2006

241   Liz Johnson, Buffalo, N.Y. 2004-2005

240   Jodi Musto, Schenectady, N.Y. 1998-1999

238   Teri Haefke, Youngstown, Oh. 2003-2004

237   Marla Chicase, Poland, Oh. 2001-2002

Individual Three-Game Series

Men

900   Jeremy Sonnenfeld, Lincoln, Neb. Feb. 2, 1997

Tony Raventini, Milwaukee, Wisc. Nov. 9,1998

Vince Wood, Moreno Valley, Calif. Sept. 29, 1999

Robby Portalatin, Jackson, Mich. Dec. 28, 2000

James Hylton, Salem, Ore. May 2, 2001

Jeff Campbell II, New Castle, Pa. June 12, 2004

Darren Pomije, New Prague, Minn. Dec 9, 2004

Robert Mushtare, Fort Drum, N.Y., Dec. 3, 2005

Lonnie Billiter Jr., Fairfield, Ohio, Feb.13, 2006.

Robert Mushtare, Fort Drum, N.Y., Feb. 19, 2006

Mark Wukoman, Greenfield, Wisc., April 22, 2006

Women

878   Karen Rosenburg, Rolla, Mo. Dec. 12, 2001

877   Jackie Mitskavich, Van Wert, Ohio. Aug. 10, 1997

869   Missy Bellinder, San Diego, Calif., June 22, 2002

868   Carolyn Key-Reed, Buffalo, N.Y. March 4, 2003

867   Shannon Duplantis, New Orleans, La. July 17, 2000

Male Youth

888   Brent Arcement, Kenner, La. Jan. 20, 1990

879   Jacob Peters, Decatur, Ill. April 27, 2005

878   Jason Johnson, Novi, Mich. Dec. 7, 1993

Travis Papp, Granite City, Ill. March 8, 2001
Shawn Maldanado, Houston, Tex. May 26, 2002

Female Youth

843   Emily Snyder, Whitehall, Pa. Jan. 23, 2000
       Jessica Worsley, Lakewood, N.J. March 29, 2003
841   Clarissa Missler, Essexville, Mich. Feb. 29, 2004
838   Kelle Renniger, Williamsport, Pa. Nov. 20, 1994
836   Lindsey Coulles, Huber Heights, Oh. June 5, 2005

Five-Player Team Three-Game Series

Men

3,934   Limo Exchange, New Castle, Del. April 1, 2004
3,905   Print Mark Industries, Wilkes-Barre, Pa. Feb. 10, 2001
3,897   Westgate. Grand Rapids, Mich. Dec. 20, 2004
3,870   Just-Us Tree Service, Toledo, Ohio. May 1, 1999
3,868   Hurst Bowling Supplies, Luzerne, Pa. Feb. 23, 1994
         180 Energy Drink, Cahokia, Ill. Oct. 11, 2001
3,863   Hayward's Pro Shot, Temperence, Mich. May 12,2000
3,858   Budweiser, St. Louis, Mo. March 12, 1958

Women

3,600   All-Star Grill, Livonia, Mich. Nov. 20, 2000
3,581   SUV's, Wichita, Kan. Nov. 18, 2001
3,557   Turbo 2-N-1 Grips/Remerica Realtors, Detroit, Mich. 4-10-2000
3,553   Abie's Ladies, Lansing, Mich. Oct. 28, 2003
3,552   Contour Power Grips, West Bloomfield, Mich. March 14, 1998
         Sun & Company, Tonawanda, N.Y. May 12, 1999

Five-Player Team Game

Men

1,413   O.T. Hills, St. Charles, Mo. Feb. 15, 2001
1,410   Golden Harvest No. 4, Springfield, Ill. May 1, 1993
1,403   Jukebox Junction, Sherman, Ill. Nov. 14, 1997
1,394   St. Clair Lanes, St. Clairsville, Ohio. Feb. 3, 2001
1,391   Pepper Nik's, Fond du Lac, Wisc. April 15, 1999

Women

1,318   Contour Power Grips, West Bloomfield, Mich. March 14, 1998
1,303   All-Star Grill, Belleville, Mich. April 10, 2000
1,294   Hamtrack Singles/Hi Tech, Livonia, Mich. April 10, 2000
1,292   Women's Central State Tournament, Akron, Ohio. March 2, 1994
1,291   Lefties Plus, Boise, Idaho. April 10, 1999

300 Games, Career

Men
83	Jeff Carter, Springfield, Ill
75	Joe Jimenez, Saginaw, Mich.
	Dean Wolf, Reading, Pa.
71	Chris Hayward, Toledo, Ohio.
	Jeff Ripic, Endicott, N.Y.
70	Jerry Kessler, Dayton, Ohio.
	Frank Massengale Jr., Hixon, Tenn.

Male Youth
27	P.J. Haggerty, Weimar, Calif.
23	Rory Kalanquin, Davison, Mich
	Steve Novak, Oceanside, N.Y.
	Sean Rash, Anchorage, Alaska.
20	Mason Sherman, Moorpark, Calif.

Women
35	Tish Johnson, Northridge, Calif.
	Jodi Musto, Schenectady, N.Y.
34	Altramese Webb, Detroit, Mich.
29	Dede Davidson, Woodland Hills, Calif.
27	Aleta Sill, Dearborn, Mich.

Female Youth
8	Jackie Edwards, Simi Valley, Calif.
7	Jeannette Menacho, Rancho Cordova, Calif.
6	Marie Hollingsworth, San Leandro, Calif.

800 Series, Career

Men
94	John Chacko Jr., Larksville, Pa.
60	Gordon Childers, Benton, Ark.
58	Jerry Kessler, Dayton, Ohio
	Frank Massengale Jr., Hixon, Tenn.
	Warren Tom Wasson, Garland, Tex.

Male Youth
11	Derek Roseberry, Louisville, Ky.
	P.J. Haggerty, Weimar, Calif.

Women
15	Anne Marie Duggan, Edmond, Okla.

14　　Leanne Barrette, Pleasanton, Calif.
13　　Jodi Musto, Schenectady, N.Y.
　　　Altramese Webb, Detroit, Mich.
12　　Tiffany Stanbrough, Oklahoma City, Okla.
Female Youth
3　　　Amie Willett, San Leandro, Calif.
　　　Marie Hollingsworth, San Leandro, Calif.

MALE STATE & PROVINCIAL ALL-TIME RECORDS

The following are the highest three-game individual series, five-man team game and series by men in each state and Canadian province according to USBC records through the 2004-2005 season:

State	Score	Name, Site, Date
Alabama	878	Ben Thames, Enterprise, 7-7-2003
	1,321	Adventure Travel, Mobile, 11-1-1994
	3,587	Cho Hwa #5, Huntsville, 11-22-2001
Alaska	855	Steven Brown, Anchorage, 11-20-2003
		Sean Pratt, Anchorage, 4-14-2005
	1,323	The Wilson Agency, Anchorage, 4-16-2003
	3,633	The Wilson Agnecy, Anchorage, 4-16-2003
Arizona	875	Rich Kenny, Mesa, 8-13-2005
	1,334	World Wide Water Systems, 10-14-1999
	3,707	Team Jab, Mesa, 3-2-2003
Arkansas	886	Michael Belcher, Fort Smith, 2-24-1999
	1,326	Enterprise Lanes, Enterprise, 5-18-2004
	3,809	Watson Pool & Spa, Benton, 2-27-2003
California	900	Vince Wood, Moreno Valley, 9-29-1999
	1,344	Madruga Iron Works, Tracy, 4-6-1989
	3,769	Williamson Shell, Sacramento, 3-15-1973
Colorado	888	Tony Passarelli, Greely, 4-2-2000
	1,323	El Napal Restaurant, Colorado Springs, 2-17-1997
	3,674	Western Bowlers Assn., Lakewood, 4-19-1991
Connecticut	886	Christopher Marchand, Groton, 12-22-1998
	1,353	Tollman Spring, East Hartford, 11-9-2004
	3,655	Ken Dunbar's Pro Shop, Woodbridge, 2-1-1996
Delaware	899	Ron Prettyman, Claymont, 2-10-1996
	1,371	Limo Exchange, New Castle, 4-1-2004
	3,934	Limo Exchange, New Castle, 4-1-2004

Florida	886	Bill Connors Jr., Lakeland, 10-28-2004
	1,380	Non-Dairy Creamers, Boca Raton, 12-23-2004
	3,819	Lou Scalia's Pro Shop, Tamarac, 2-4-2003
Georgia	887	Bret Dal Santo, Savannah, 10-25-1990
	1,300	Yeah Baby, Norcross, 9-21-2004
	3,619	Strikers Reloaded, Rome, 10-14-2003
Hawaii	875	Daniel Maglangit, Ewa Beach, 3-8-1982
	1,316	Love's Ltd., Honolulu, 3-21-1969
	3,791	Love's Ltd., Honolulu, 3-21-1969
Idaho	876	Michael Tackett, Twin Falls, 2-5-2003
	1,332	Allsport Trophy, Boise, 3-9-2005
	3,569	Moore's Machine, Boise, 12-29-2004
Illinois	884	Dave Coufal, Lyons, 2-28-2001
	1,410	Golden Harvest #4, Springfield, 5-1-1993
	3,858	180 Energy Drink, Cahokia, 10-11-2001
Indiana	890	Lou Gorcos, Michigan City, 8-14-2000
	1,378	Team Sims, Portage, 3-4-2004
	3,820	Randy Harvey's Pro Shop, Elkhart,12-23-2003
Iowa	878	Neil Greenwald Jr., Muscatine, 10-21-1995
		Pat Reisinger, Cedar Rapids, 2/28-2001
	1,380	Phil & Larry's Saloon, Davenport, 3-4-2004
	3,798	Frank's Pro Shop, Waterloo, 4-17-2003
Kansas	889	Ed Henning, Wichita, 3-28-2005
	1,382	Sunset Bowl, Kansas City, 9-8-1987
	3,718	Gregg Security, Pittsburg, 9-5-1982
Kentucky	879	Kenny Stephens, Lexington, 2-21-2005
	1,368	Garretts Five, Louisville, 2-21-2004
	3,777	Cardinal Force, Louisville, 10-9-1996
Louisiana	888	Brent Arcement (YABA), Kenner, 1-20-1990
	1,299	B&D Pro Shop, Kenner, 10-29-1992
	3,731	Fence Jumpers, Harahan, 8-30-2004
Maine	856	Joseph Ramsdell, III, Waterville, 3-18-2003
	1,298	Ball Doctor's Pro Shop, Waverville, 2-28-2001
	3,632	Focused 5, Portland, 2-8-2003
Maryland	878	Wayne Webb, Middle River, 3-2-1991
	1,343	Action Auto Center, Baltimore, 3-28-1991
	3,782	Balls Deep, Middle River, 2-21-2003
Massachusetts	883	Michael Fabian, North Attleboro, 4-16-2003

	1,296	Titleist 1, New Bedford, 12-31-1995
	3,695	Send It, Somerset, 11-14-2000
Michigan	900	Robby Portalatin, Jackson, 12-28-2000
	1,366	Booth Radiator, Muskegon, 3-31-2001
		#17 Young & Old, Warren, 1-2-2001
	3,897	Westgate Bowl, Grandville, 12-20-2004
Minnesota	900	Darren Pomije, New Progue, 12-9-2004
	1,381	Bell Manufacturing, St. Paul, 2-4-1999
	3,807	Breakpoint Pro Shop, Sartell, 1-9-04
Mississippi	857	Will Mills, New Albany, 2-27-2005
	1,335	Panorama Lanes, Mehlville, 12-12-1984
	3,715	Rock's Ice, Gauthier, 9-30-1997
Missouri	898	Alonzo Spiller, Kansas City, 10-19-2000
	1,413	O.T. Hills, St. Charles, 2-15-2002
	3,858	Budweiser Beer, St. Louis, 3-12-1958
Montana	862	Jim Potvin Jr., Anaconda, 3-6-2001
	1,273	Bound for Glory, Helena, 5-1-1993
	3,588	Montana Jerky Co., Kalispell, 5-18-1996
Nebraska	900	Jeremy Sonnenfield, Lincoln, 2-2-1977
	1,361	Old Milwaukee, Norfolk, 12-19-1990
	3,654	Bowler's Choice Pro Shop, Omaha, 11-16-1997
Nevada	878	Phillip Platko, Las Vegas, 10-12-1999
	1,214	Reno All-Stars, Reno, 5-22-1982
	3,404	Reno All-Stars, Reno, 5-22-1982
New Hampshire	880	Richard Hussey Jr., Clermont, 3-30-1994
	1,259	Bowl Pro Sales, Dover, 3-15-2005
	3,446	Barns of Bradford, Manchester, 10-28-1992
New Jersey	899	Tom Jordan, Union, 3-7-1989
		Mike Reasoner, Old Bridge, 7-26-1999
		Orville Johnson, Bridgeton, 5-13-2005
	1,350	V. Loria & Sons, Paramus, 4-23-1979
	3,754	Faber Cement, Teaneck, 2-25-1982
New Mexico	877	Joe Sanburn, Albuquerque, 3-30-1994
		Wade Sellers, Albuquerque, 1-30-2003
	1,271	Leisure Bowl, Albuquerque, 1975
	3,599	Enterprise Video, Albuquerque, 5-5-1989
New York	898	William Young, Homer, 12-8-2004
	1,371	Concord Pools, Scotia, 3-6-1995

	3,813	Vince Gance Agency, Endicott, 2-18-1993
North Carolina	880	Kenneth McNeely Jr., Morgantown, 5-15-1996
	1,349	Minnesota Timberwolves, Ashville, 10-31-1995
	3,664	Big Daddy's Crew, Raleigh 12-9-2004
North Dakota	859	Casey Dodgson, Jamestown, 12-1-2004
	1,301	Stoves Plus, Williston, 10-31-2002
	3,645	Midway Lanes, Mandan, 3-22-1987
Ohio	899	Steve Lewis, Xenia, 9-19-1996
	1,394	St. Clair Bowl, St. Clairsville, 2-3-2001
	3,870	Just-Us Tree Service, Toledo, 5-1-1999
Oklahoma	878	Charles McLean, Oklahoma City, 9-2-1997
	1,360	Team Divided, Yukon, 5-6-2004
	3,764	Came From Behind, Edmond, 10-9-2002
Oregon	900	James Hylton, Salem, 5-2-2001
	1,347	Team Storm, Portland, 4-19-2003
	3,689	Dream Team, Pendleton, 2-2-1991
Pennsylvania	900	Jeff Campbell II, New Castle, 6-12-2004
	1,379	Laurento's Barbershop, Blue Ball, 12-23-2003
	3,905	Print Mark Industries, Wilkes-Barre, 2-10-2001
Rhode Island	889	Bob D'Antuono, Lincoln, 3-5-1997
	1,281	Video Guild, Westerly, 11-2-1995
	3,661	Strike Force, Westerly, 9-24-1998
South Carolina	884	Blais Mascitelli, Spartanburg, 12-11-1990
	1,301	Solid 9, Greenwood, 11-17-2004
	3,680	H+B Ball Factory, Greenville, 4-13-1997
South Dakota	865	Shon Phillips, Winner, 3-5-2004
	1,267	Top Line Bowling Supply, Sioux Falls, 1-18-1973
	3,549	Edwards Construction, Vermillion, 2-15-2001
Tennessee	879	Billy Moss, Hermitage, 2-18-2002
	1,328	B&H Vending, Nashville, 11-20-1989
	3,746	Get You Summa That, Nashville, 10-6-1997
Texas	890	Frankie Alonzo, Desoto, 4-26-2002
	1,360	NBMFS, Dallas, 2005-2006.
Utah	887	Russ Hunt, N. Salt Lake City, 3-18-1996
	1,298	Walt Palmer Supply Co., Salt Lake City, 4-4-1996
	3,572	Hilltop Lanes, Salt Lake City, 4-11-1997
Vermont	888	Jonathan Wilbur, Rutland, 3-6-2004
	1,298	Millenium Lawn Care, Shelbourne, 11-4-2002

	3,629	Interstate Battery, Rutland, 12-4-2003
Virginia	878	Paul Rumbaugh II, 6-29-2005
	1,384	Steve's Delivery, Richmond, 10-25-1995
	3,757	Strike Factory Pro Shop, Fredericksburg, 9-26-2000
Washington	889	David Childers, Vancover, 4-12-2002
	1,328	New Frontier Lanes, Tacoma, 2-14-1992
	3,619	Kenmore Village Lanes, Tacoma, 1972
West Virginia	876	Jeff Germann, Wheeling, 12-18-2002
	1,294	Ball Dogs, Parkersburg, 10-15-1999
	3,654	5-Man, Parkersburg, 5-21-1988
Wisconsin	900	Tony Roventini, Milwaukee, 11-8-1999
	1,391	Pepper Nik's, Fond du Lac, 4-13-1999
	3,810	Visionary Bowling Products, Racine, 5-5-2002
Wyoming	858	Ivan Weitz, Cheyenne, 2-3-1994
		Justin More (YABA), Cheyenne, 4-9-1994
	1,268	Toastmaster Bar, Green River, 2-18-2002
	3,523	Toastmaster Bar, Green River, 10-8-2001

CANADA

Province	Score	Name, Site, Date
Alberta	794	Joe Lagadyn, Edmonton, 11-15-1984
		Not listed
		Not listed
British Columbia	856	Cal Smith, Vancover, 3-24-1988
		Not listed
		Not listed
Manitoba	834	Stewart MacKenzie, Winnipeg, 3-10-2000
	1,123	Turret, Winnipeg, 1934
	3,261	Turret, Winnipeg, 1934
New Brunswick	877	Eddie Zoellner, Richibucton, 12-16-2000
		Not listed
		Not listed
Ontario	869	Robert Woolley, Sault Ste. Marie, 4-10-1996
	1,295	All-Star Pro Shop, Windsor, 12-12-1994
	3,646	Johnny Shotz, Windsor, 12-9-1999
Quebec	879	Guillaume Nadeau, St. Foy, 10-30-2001
		Not listed
		Not listed

Saskatchewan 782   Daryle Day, Regina, 4-24-1988
                            Not listed
                            Not listed

FEMALE STATE & PROVINCIAL ALL-TIME RECORDS

The following are the highest three-game individual series, five-man team game and series by women in each state and Canadian province according to USBC records through the 2004-2005 season:

State	Score	Name, Site, Date
Alabama	837	Wendy MacPherson, Huntsville, 2-11-1998
	Not listed	
	3,144	Randy & Rick's Pro Shop, Birmingham, 1996
Alaska	823	Jennifer Barron, Anchorage, 8-22-1995
	1,047	Flintstones (city and date not listed)
	Not listed	
Arizona	847	Marcia Kamrowski, Phoenix, 7-12-2000
	1,113	Wayne's Landscaping, Phoenix, 1993
	3,158	Wayne's Landscaping, Phoenix, 1993
Arkansas	847	Tiffany Stanbrough, N. Little Rock, 10-12-2003
	Not listed	
	Not listed	
California	869	Missy Bellinder, San Diego, 6-22-2002
	1,194	Punami Power, Chino Hills, 10-29-1998
	3,499	Punami Power, Chino Hills, 1-15-1998
Colorado	845	Tamara Pike, Lakewood, 4-10-2002
	1,168	Champions Pro Shop, Colorado Springs, 10-21-2003
	3,347	Us and Them, Denver, 1990
Connecticut	835	Jennifer Swanson, Milford, 2-26-2004
	1,047	We Blow Doors (city and date not listed)
	3,003	Free Flying Five, Hartford, 1984
Delaware	848	Patricia Renshaw, Wilmington, 1-24-1996
	Not listed	
	Not listed	
Florida	844	Kay Boswell, Tampa, 1-30-2000
	1,132	JSBMC, Broward County, 1995
	3,211	Boo's Bowlers, Tampa, 1996
Georgia	845	Christine Rumph, Valdosta, 4-3-2003

	Not listed	
	Not listed	
Hawaii	803	Linda Painter, Barber Point, 1993
	Not listed	
	Not listed	
Idaho	844	Jackie Thomas, Boise, 3-4-1998
	1,291	Lefties Plus, Boise, 4-10-1999
	Not listed	
Illinois	858	Eula Ivy, Bellwood, 8-1-2003
	1,231	Carter Brothers Lumber, Springfield, 11-4-1997
	3,508	Carter Brothers Lumber, Springfield, 10-28-1997
Indiana	866	Jada Mocaby, Hobart, 1-27-2004
	1,228	Tatone's, Hobart, 1996
	3,457	J&L Fasteners, Highland, 10-17-2003
Iowa	836	Tricia Nederhiser, Cedar Rapids, 2-25-2005
	1,095	Dilts Trucking, Council Bluffs, 1985
	3,115	Sammy G. Lanes, Davenport-Bettendorf, 1993
Kansas	860	Maggie Crawford, Topeka, 3-12-2003
	1,215	SUVs, Wichita, 11-18-2001
	3,581	SUVs, Wichita, 11-18-2001
Kentucky	829	Melinda Johnson, Lexington, 10-20-2003
	1,115	Pat's Girls, Floyd-Pike counties, 1993
	Not listed	
Louisiana	867	Shannon Duplantis, Kenner, 7-27-2000
	1,178	Sugar Bowl, New Orleans, 1995
Maine	784	Brenda Hoyt, Portland, 4-6-2003
	Not listed	
Maryland	835	Terri Bollinger, Baltimore, 11-9-2003
	Not listed	
	Not listed	
Massachusetts	826	Mary Marois, Gardner, 4-20-2005
	Not listed	
	Not listed	
Michigan	865	Jeanette Betts, Saginaw, 10-16-1997
	1,328	Contour Power Grips, Detroit, 3-14-1998
	3,600	All-Star Grill, Livonia, 11-20-2000
Minnesota	859	Patty Ann, New Ulm, 1984-1985
	1,252	River Liquors, Minneapolis, 1995

	3,477	Linds/On Track, St. Paul, 11-4-2001
Missouri	878	Karen Rosenburg, Rolla, 12-12-2001
	1,262	Drug Package Inc., St. Louis, 1993
	3,446	Drug Pakage Inc., St. Louis, 1993
Mississippi	823	Judy Vogel, Piscayne, 9-15-1999
	1,176	Here Barely, Gautier, 1996
	Not listed	
Montana	812	Fawn Lyons, Butte, 1-31-1996
	1,032	Skyway Bowl Follies, Great Falls, 1990
	2,830	Spare Parts, Great Falls, 1993
Nebraska	837	Cynthia Kesterson, Papillion, 5-3-1992
	1,207	Thunderbowl II, Omaha, 1-2-1999
	3,466	Strike More Spareless, Grand Falls, 1997
Nevada	835	Cynthia Abasta, Reno, 10-18-1996
	1,074	South Pacific, Las Vegas, 1968-1969
	3,040	210 Strikes, Carson City, 1996-1997
New Hampshire	771	Mary Ellen Thorne, Nashua, 1997
	915	Bowlers Annex, Merrimack ,(date not listed)
	2,681	Let It Be, Merrimack, (date not listed)
New Jersey	855	Christine Mackenhaupt, Oakland, 3-30-2005
	1,146	Joe Tolvay's Pro Shop, Bergen County, 1986
	3,378	Canadian Club, Kenilworth, 1983-1984
New Mexico	833	Dana Miller-Mackie, Albuquerque, 3-20-1995
	1,199	Silvis Lanes, Albequerque, 6-21-1998
	3,335	Silvis Lanes, Albequerque, 6-21-1998
New York	868	Jodi Musto, Latham, 1-25-1995
		Carolyn Key-Reed, Buffalo, 3-4-2003
	1,238	Brockport Bowl Grabpa Ladies Travel, Brockport, 12-17-1998
	3,548	Sue & Company, Buffalo, 5-12-1999
North Carolina	848	Sammi Byrd, Fayetteville, 6-13-2005
	1,068	The Bowling Center, Wilmington, 1986
	Not listed	
North Dakota	846	Missy Miller, Bismarck, 10-1-1998
	Not listed	
	Not listed	
Ohio	877	Jackie Mitskavich, Van Wert, 8-10-1997

	1,292	Women's Central State Assn. Tournament, Akron, 3-2-1994
	3,416	Plaza Lanes, Dayton, 1997
Oklahoma	831	Nancy Johnson, Tulsa, 12-10-1990
	1,135	Penn 44 Pro Shop, Oklahoma City, 1986
	Not listed	
Oregon	826	Stacey Garman, Portland, 11-4-2004
	1,189	Bowler's Performance Center, Portland, 1993
	3,405	Bowler's Performance Center, Portland, 1993
Pennsylvania	845	Jen Oleniak, Wilkes-Barre, 12-9-2001
	1,226	Sheraton Inn, Scranton, 1981-1982
		Veltri & Sons Clothier, Scranton, 1984-1985
	3,307	Tetterton's Pro Shop, Reading, 1990
Rhode Island	823	Melanie Bennett, Cranston, 3-17-2002
	Not listed	
	Not listed	
South Carolina	847	Jodi Hughes, Spartanburg, 4-11-1995
	1,067	Gutter Babes, Spartanburg, 6-8-1996
	2,859	Gutter Babes, Spartanburg, 6-8-1996
South Dakota	835	Ranae Janssen, Sioux Falls, 10-11-1996
		Debby Slusser, Rapid City, 1-31-2002
	Not listed	
	Not listed	
Tennessee	836	Terri Layne, Hixon, 4-23-2003
	Not listed	
	Not listed	
Texas	865	Anne Marie Duggan, Dallas, 7-16-1993
	1,206	Oakheaven Animal Clinic, Fort Worth, 1990-1991
	3,177	Twacy-N-Da-Supwemes, San Antonio, 1993
Utah	827	Karen Pullman, Salt Lake City, 4-4-2001
	Not listed	
	2,957	McIntyre Center, Salt Lake City, 1984
Vermont	816	Cathy Turner, Brattleboro, 6-18-2001
	Not listed	
	Not listed	
Virginia	832	Carla Galzerano, Mechanicsville, 5-2-1999
	Not listed	
	Not listed	

Washington	838	Kristy Whitcher, Bremerton, 9-11-1997
	1,235	North Bowl, Spokane, 11-2-1999
	3,151	Daffodil $1111 Invitational, Valley, 1993
West Virginia	836	Diana Howard, Dunbar, 9-23-03
	1,246	Devault's Pro Shop, Weirton, 4-15-2004
	Not listed	
Wisconsin	864	Diane Guttormsen Northern, Kenosha, 1996
	1,284	Ber Ben Rec, Green Bay, 12-19-1995
	3,486	Brunswick/KR Strikeforce, Milwaukee, 3-27-2004
Wyoming	824	Alice Moon, Casper, 3-20-2004
	Not listed	
	Not listed	

CANADA

Province	**Score**	**Name, Site, Date**
Alberta		None listed
British Columbia	786	Nancy Yven, Richmond, 3-26-2003
	Not listed	
	Not listed	
Manitoba	None listed	
Ontario	804	Joanne Keefe, Sarina, 1991
	1,173	Angie's Fashions, Windsor, 3-27-2001
	3,228	Angie's Fashions, Windsor, 3-27-2001
Quebec	816	Isabelle Rioux, Trois Rivieres, 3-25-2002
	Not listed	
	Not listed	
Saskatchewan	None listed	

By the Numbers

ALL SPARES: The least you can score with an all spares game is 100, while the most you can score without getting a strike is 190. To get a 100 you have to throw a gutter ball on the first ball in each of the last nine frames and then throw a strike for your spare, while to score a 190 you have to get nine pins on the first ball of each of the last nine frames and pick up the one-pin spare.

BOWLER'S DICTIONARY

In many ways bowling has a language of its own. Here are some of the most used terms you will hear in today's bowling centers:

Address – The bowler's starting position. "He has a good address, but he is too fast on the approach."

Aim – Referring to the method a bowler uses to direct the bowling ball to the pins. Bowlers use a variety of aiming methods including spot bowling, line bowling, area bowling and pin bowling. "Take aim before you throw."

Alley or Allies – An old name for the actual bowling surface. In plural it refers to a set of bowling surfaces, or to the entire bowling establishment. Bowlers often use the singular as a plural in saying "I'm going to the bowling alley." Today, most bowlers call the bowling surface a lane, and the set of surfaces the lanes. "I like lane nine best at Quality Lanes."

Approach – Section of the lane covering the back edge to the foul line. Approaches are between 15 feet long (USBC minimum) and 16 feet and are used by bowlers to walk to the foul line to release the ball. Approach is also used to refer to the way the bowler walks to the foul line to release the ball. "The guy uses all of the approach." "She has a sound approach."

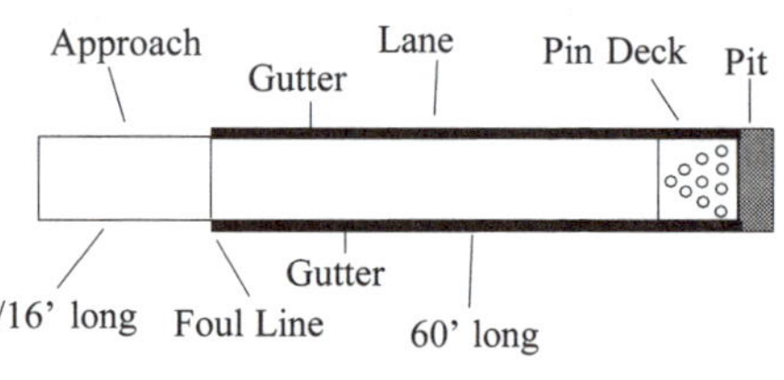

Anchor – The last bowler in the lineup of a team. The anchor on most teams is the bowler with the highest average. "Joe is the anchor for our team."

Angle – Direction the ball travels into the pocket. "His ball angle is really sharp."

Area Bowling – The bowler uses a general area as a target to direct the ball to the pins. Bowlers who throw sweeping curves and sharp hooks often try to roll the ball over a particular area about three-quarters down the lane where they hope the ball will begin its path to the 1-3 or 1-2 pocket. "I don't aim for a particular spot, I shoot for an area."

Arm swing – Usually refers to the bowler's total arm motion before the ball is released. Good bowlers tend to have a smooth, relaxed arm swing. Back swing, movement of the arm behind the bowler, is a part of the total arm swing. "Gloria is consistent with her arm swing, which is part of the reason she has good scores."

Arrows – The arrow-like marks on the lanes located about 10 feet beyond the foul line. Most lanes have an arrow exactly in line with the head pin and three arrows on each side of the lane at the five, 10 and 15 boards. Bowlers use the marks to aim for the pins. "Bill hits that third arrow every time."

Average – Bowler's averages are determined by adding their individual game scores and dividing that total by the number of games they bowled. If Joe bowls six games and the total of all those games is 1,110 pins, his average of 185 is determined by dividing six into 1,110. If Mary bowls 18 games and her total of all game scores is 3,060 she can determine her average by dividing 3,060 by 18. "What's her average?"

Baby Split – Usually refers to a leave of the 2 and 7 pins or the 3 and 10 pins. "He had a baby split in the eighth frame."

Backup Ball – A ball released in such as way as to curve to the right for right-handed bowlers and to the left for left-handed bowlers. It is generally regarded as a poor way to bowl. It is caused when right handed bowlers release the ball with the wrist turned to right and when left handed bowlers release the ball with the wrist turned to the left. "I wish he would get rid of that backup ball, and learn to thrown a hook."

Back Swing -- Portion of the bowler's delivery from the time the ball descends from the start position past the leg to a point behind the bowler where the ball reaches an apex and begins the forward swing toward the lane and pins. "Jean would bowl better if she had a more natural back swing."

Beer frame – Usually the fifth frame. Teams create ways to get a teammate to buy drinks in this frame for the rest of the team. One method teams use to "pick" the buyer is to assess the player who has the worst score or scores least in the fifth frame. "It's the beer frame, you better strike.

Bevel -- Rounded edge of finger holes and thumb holes in a bowling ball. "The beveled edges should make it easier on your fingers."

Blind – The spot in the lineup not filled, either because a regular bowler is absent, or the team does not have a full squad. The blind spot is usually assessed a score for handicap purposes of the bowlers average minus 10 pins or a standard 140 for men and 120 for women. "Their team is bowling with a blind."

Board – Each bowling lane is composed of 40 to 41 boards one-inch wide across it. The boards may be made of wood (maple and pine) or a synthetic material that looks like wood. Players usually aim by starting with their feet on particular boards and delivering the ball over particular boards. "Tammy consistently throws down the 12-board."

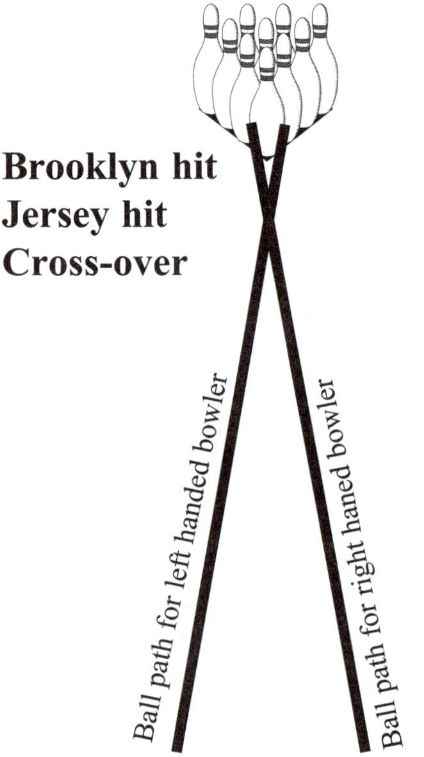

Break Point -- The place on the lanes where the ball makes its greatest change in direction. "Earl's break point is usually at the five or six board about five feet in front of the head pin."

Brooklyn – A strike achieved by hitting left of the head pin in the 1-2 pocket rather than right of the head pin in the 1-3 pocket by a right-handed bowler. A Brooklyn is also referred to as a "Jersey" and a "crossover" strike. Left-handed bowlers can "crossover" to the 1-3 pocket for a strike, but that is not a Brooklyn or a Jersey. "One of Pat's three strikes was a Brooklyn."

Carry – The number of pins knocked down by the ball and moving pins. When a number of pins are struck and knocked down by other pins it is called "good carry." "Wow! Bob had good carry on that ball."

Carry Down -- Oil that is moved from the front part of the lanes to the rear of the lanes by passing bowling balls. "Whenever there is a lot of carry down, bowlers have to adjust their lines to the pocket."

Channel – The depressed area on each side of the lane. It is usually 9 to 10 inches wide. It is also called the gutter. "Rob throws more balls in the channel than anyone on his team."

Chop – Hitting and knocking one or two pins down while just missing the other pin. "She had a mean chop miss on that 2-4-5 spare shot."

Conventional Grip -- A ball drilled so the bowler can grip it by placing his/her fingers in the ball to the second joint, and can place his/her entire thumb in thumb hole. "Ed prefers a ball with a conventional grip."

Conversion – Making the spare. Bowlers also pick up the spare. "Shirley had a good conversion in the ninth frame."

Count – The number of pins a bowler gets on the ball after a spare. In scoring rules, a spare is computed as 10 pins plus the number of pins — count or fill — knocked down on the next ball. The term count is often called fill. "Come on John, get a good count."

Cranker -- A bowler (usually younger) who generates high speed and numerous revolutions on the ball by using maximum back swing and a cupped delivery. "Crankers can really slam the pins."

Curve Ball – A ball that breaks in a big arc from right to left for a right-handed bowler, and from left to right for a left-handed bowler. A hook breaks in the same direction, but much sharper. "Doug throws a strong curve."

Deck – The end of the lane where the pins are located when standing. "Those pins were sliding all over the deck."

Deflection -- The amount of change in a bowling ball's path or trajectory caused by hitting the pins. "Mary throws a 10-pound ball, so the deflection of her ball is quite noticeable."

Double – Hitting two strikes in a row. "Bill is on a double."

Double wood – When one pin is directly behind another pin in a spare attempt. Double-wood leaves are the 1-5, 2-8 and 3-9. The leave is also called sleeper, barmaid or one-in-the-dark. "You usually have to hit that double-wood solid to pick it up." 

Down and In – A pattern of throwing the ball straight down the lane so it hooks into the pocket just before reaching the pins. Curve ball bowlers throw out and in. "Jesse used to have a great down-and-in shot."

Dutch 200 – A score of exactly 200 made by posting alternate strikes and spares throughout a single game. A Dutch 200 may be started with a strike or a spare, as long as they are alternated through the entire game. "He rolled a Dutch 200 and won a bowling patch from the United States Bowling Congress."

Name	1	2	3	4	5	6	7	8	9	10
Dan Barry	20	40	60	80	100	120	140	160	180	200

Fast lane – Some bowlers call a fast lane one with a lot of oil that makes it more difficult to throw a hook, while some bowlers say it is the opposite, a dry lane that allows for big curves and diving hooks. "The lanes are fast tonight."

Fill – The number of pins a bowler gets on the ball after a spare. In scoring rules, a spare is computed as 10 pins plus the number of pins — fill or count — knocked down on the next ball. The term fill is often called count. "Come on John, we need a good fill on this ball."

Fingertip Grip -- Ball drilled so the bowler grips it by inserting his/her fingers into the holes to the first joint, and can insert his/her entire thumb in the thumb hole. "Most bowlers today use a fingertip grip ball."

Five-bagger – Registering five strikes in a row. "Five baggers are great for your bowling score."

Follow Through – Arm motion during and immediately after the ball is released. Usually the arm is extended out and up in a good follow through after the ball is released. "The best bowlers have a strong follow through."

Foul – Touching any surface beyond the foul line while delivering the ball. When a bowler fouls he or she gets zero for that part of the frame. If a bowler fouls on the first ball, pins are re-racked, and the bowler can get no more than a spare on the second ball. If a foul occurs on a bowler's second ball, the bowler gets no score for that ball and gets only the number of pins knocked down on the first ball as a score. "Gene had a foul in the ninth frame. That really hurt."

Foul Line – Line at the end of the approach dividing the approach and the beginning of the lane. Bowlers may not touch any part of the lane beyond the foul line without loss of score on that particular ball. Foul lines are covered by an electronic beam which when broken calls a foul on the bowler. "Whatever you do in the last frame, don't hit the foul line."

Foundation – A strike in the ninth frame. The ninth frame is also called the foundation frame. "Okay June, get a good foundation for the 10th."

Frame – The tenth part of a game. Each bowling game has 10 frames. "Hank rolled three strikes to win the game in the 10th frame."

Gutter – Same as the lane channel. "Maranda throws her ball in the gutter so much she thinks it's the only way to throw a straight ball."

Gutter Ball – A ball rolled into the channel. When a ball is thrown into the channel, it becomes a dead ball, and scores no pins even if it should bounce out and hit pins on its way to the pit at the end of the lane. "It is not unusual to throw a gutter ball when trying to pickup the 10-pin."

Handicap – Number of pins awarded to bowlers based on their averages. Leagues use a variety of handicapping methods. "The Sunday night mixed league is a handicap league."

Head Pin – The number one pin in the 10-pin arrangement. "It's pretty tough to get a strike if you miss the head pin."

Heads -- First 20-foot section of the lanes beyond the foul line. This section gets the hardest ware as it is where most of the balls are placed. Bowlers often refer to the heads breaking down, which means the usual amount of oil placed on this section is picked up by bowling balls, making the section dryer than usual. In natural lanes this section would be made of hard maple.

Heavy Hit -- A pocket shot that hits more of the head pin than an ideal shot. "That was a heavy hit, but it still paid."

Hole – The 1-3 pocket for a right-handed bowler, and 1-2 pocket for a lefty. "He hit the hole in every frame."

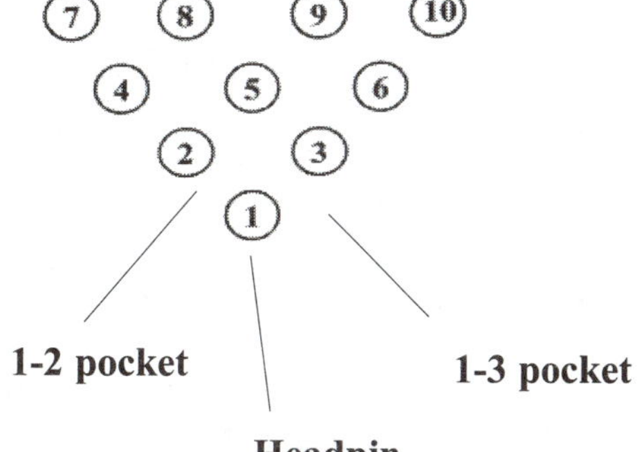

Hook Ball – A ball that breaks sharply to the left for a right handed bowler and sharply to the right for a left-handed bowler. Most hook balls are thrown down and in, while curve balls are thrown out and in. According to studies, balls entering the pockets at sharper angles as in a hook register more strikes than balls entering the pockets with less angle. "Old Andy could throw a hook ball across two lanes."

Inside -- The middle 20 boards of a lane. "Steve always plays an inside line."

Jersey – A strike registered when a right-handed bowler hits the 1-2 pocket. It is also called a Brooklyn and a crossover. *(See graphic with Brooklyn explanation)* "I'll take a Brooklyn any time."

Kegler – An old term used as a synonym for bowler. Sports writers like to use the term to keep from writing bowler over and over. "The keglers had a great night Thursday at old St. John's Lanes."

Lane(s) – A lane is the playing surface for bowling, while lanes is used to refer to the bowling establishment. A bowling lane is 62' 10.75" long and 42 inches wide. The approach is another 15 to 16 feet long.   The head pin is exactly 60 feet from the foul line. "Let's go over to the lanes and throw a few games."

Lead Off – The bowler who bowls first for a team. "Marjie is our lead off bowler."

Leave – The number of pins left standing after throwing the first ball. "I had a three-pin leave, but I made the spare."

Lift – Giving the ball an upward motion with your hand and fingers at the point of release. "Jim has good lift on the ball."

Line – The path of the ball. Also a game as in "let's go to Cherryvale and bowl a line or two."

Line Bowling – When the bowler attempts to hit a particular pin or place by rolling the ball from one point on the lane to another.   "He is throwing a good line."

Lofting or Loft – Trajectory of the ball from the bowler to the lane. When a bowler has a good loft the ball is placed beyond the foul line and hits the lane smoothly. When a bowler throws the ball too high, or is lofting the ball, the ball strikes the lane with a loud sound and may damage the lane. Many bowling lanes post "no lofting" signs. "Jack has good loft on his ball." "Old Sam was thrown off the lanes for lofting his ball too much."

Mark – A strike or spare. Also the point on the lane the bowler is using as a starting place and the point out on the lane the bowler is using as a target. "Jimmy had a mark in every frame in that game." "Evelyn can hit her mark every time."

Messenger – A pin or pins that roll across the lane after most of the others have fallen. "The messenger took out the 10-pin."

Miss – When a bowler does not get all 10 pins in a particular frame. It is also referred to as an open.   "I had a miss in the fifth frame."

Mixer – A ball the causes the pins to bounce around. Mixers are usually the result of throwing a ball that had hard drive because of its revolutions toward the pins. "Karen throws a great mixer."

Nose Hit – A ball that hits full on the head pin. "A nose hit usually results in a big split."

Open – When a bowler does not get all 10 pins in a particular frame. It is also referred to as a miss. "I had an open in the fifth frame."

Open Bowling – Practice bowling. Non-league and/or non-tournament bowling. "Open bowling hours are from noon to 5 p.m. weekdays."

Out and In – Refers to a ball thrown out toward the gutter (the right for a right-hander and the left for a left-hander) that curves back toward the head pin. "Sheila sometimes throws out and in, especially when she is really bowling well."

Outside – The far left or far right side of a lane. "Dwight always goes outside with his ball."

PG – Used in some areas (mostly in the east) to describe a game in which the bowler had either a spare or strike (a mark) in every frame of a single game. "I had a PG going until I missed the five-pin in the eighth frame."

Pacers – A pacer is a bowler who fills in to balance the rotation of the teams, but whose scores do not count. Pacer situations vary depending on league rules. In many leagues, a new bowler establishing an average in a league previously started might bowl the first night as a pacer while establishing an average in that league. "Harry is going to bowl with our team tonight as a pacer."

Perfect Game – Rolling all strikes (12) in a single game to achieve a score of 300. "Gary rolled a 300 game last night at Tarpon Lanes."

Name	1	2	3	4	5	6	7	8	9	10
Darin Baginski	30	60	90	120	150	180	210	240	270	300

Pick – Same as a chop when the bowler hits only the front pin of a leave, or just gets one of two pins standing. "Joe had a pick on the 6-10 spare. He only got the six."

Picket fence – A leave of 1-2-4-7 or 1-3-6-10. It is also called a rail and railroad leave. "Tammy is shooting at the picket fence."

Pins - The wooden objects bowlers attempt to knock down with a bowling ball. In 10-pin bowling the pins are made of maple, are 15 inches in height, and must weight at least 2 pounds, 14 ounces and not more than 3 pounds, 10 ounces. They have a diameter of slightly less than 5 inches at the widest point. Pins are arranged in a triangle with a distance between each pin of 12 inches from center to center.

Pin Bowling – When a bowler aims directly at the pins or a pin. "He's a pin bowler."

Pitch – The angle at which the thumb hole and finger holes are drilled in a ball. "I don't know what the pitch is, but the pro-shop guy does."

Pocket – The areas between the one and three pins for a right-handed bowler, and between the one and two pins for a left-handed bowler. "Danny was in the pocket all night long."

Pot Game – Bowlers competing for an amount of money totaled by each contributing to the total. "Pot bowling is probably illegal in most states."

Position Round – Regular part of league season schedules when teams determined by position in the league standings compete against each other. Usually after all teams have met once in the season, the position round is scheduled where first meets second, third bowls fourth and so on. Position round schedules vary, but are most often held on the last night of the regular season. "We'll get even with you in the position round."

Punch Out – Ending the game with three consecutive strikes. "Come on Brad, we need a punch out."

Push-away – Beginning the delivery when the bowler pushes the ball out and starts walking toward the foul line. Not all bowlers have a push-away. "Some bowlers just lower the ball on their first step, but Frank has a good push-away."

Release – The hand motion used when the ball is placed on the lanes. The point in the delivery when the ball leaves the hand. "I think 99 percent of the really good bowlers have a sound release."

Reset – Setting the pins up for a second time. Bowlers can call for a reset if they think the pins are not set properly. It is each bowler's responsibility to make sure the pins are set correctly and that all 10 pins are in the rack. Occasionally, pin setting machines miss a pin and set some pins out of line. At first glance a bowler might think having one less pin would make striking easier, but usually -- especially if the middle 5-pin is missing -- pin action is less because that pin is not there to careen into other pins. According to USBC rules a dead ball is declared if "after a delivery, attention is immediately called to the fact that one or more pins were missing from the setup." "We need a reset on lane 29."

Return – The track used to deliver the ball back to the bowler from the pit. "Your ball might be stuck on the return. That happens."

Reverse – A ball thrown so it curves from left to right for a right-handed bowler and right to left for a left handed bowler. It is also called a backup ball. "I wish Mike would get rid of that backup ball."

Rotation – The number of times the ball completely rolls around its axis after it leaves the bowler's hand and rolls down the lane. A ball rolling horizontally is called rotation. "A hard hitting ball is one with good rotation."

Runway – Another term used for the 15- to 16-foot area in front of the lanes called the approach. "Don't stand around on the runway."

Sandbagger – A bowler who keeps his or her bowling average as low as possible to achieve a high handicap. "Skip is a sandbagger. He never has good scores until the second half of the season."

Scratch – No handicap. Bowlers in scratch leagues compete head to head, score to score. "The Wednesday night league is a scratch league."

Semi Finger Tip Grip -- A ball drilled so the bowler grips it by placing his/her fingers into the finger holes up to a point between the first and second finger joints, and the thumb is placed entirely in the thumb hole.

Sideboards – Walled areas on each side of the pin deck on a lane. "He picked up the 7-10 split when the 7-pin bounced off the sideboard, rolled across the deck and took out the 10."

Six-pack – Scoring six strikes in a row. "Keith has a six pack going."

Span – Distance between the finger holes and thumb hole on a bowling ball. "There was a guy named Ray in Hudson, Fla., whose span was so big it was impossible to see the finger-holes and thumb hole on his ball at the same time." 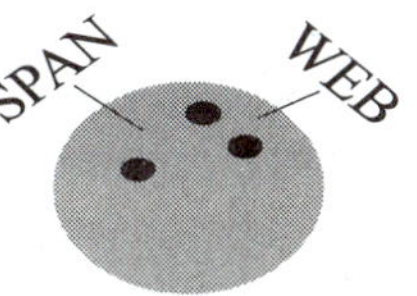

Spare – When all pins are knocked down on the second ball thrown by a bowler in a frame. A spare is scored as 10 pins plus the number of pins knocked down on the first ball in the next frame. When a spare is scored in the 10th frame, the bowler throws one more ball to complete the scoring and the game. "If you get all your spares, you will have a good game."

Split – Any combination of pins not including a head pin where there is a pin missing between pins. The 3-10 is a split. The 1-3-10 is not. "The 7-10 is the most dreaded of all splits."

Spot Bowling – Bowling to a target on the lane in trying to hit a certain area in the rack or leave. Bowlers use the arrows, spots and various colored boards for spot bowling targets. "Darwin is an exceptional spot bowler. He never misses his target."

Straight Ball – A ball thrown in a direct line toward a pin or pins. "George Billick was a definition of accuracy. He made the Bowling Hall of Fame throwing a straight ball. "

Strike – Knocking down all 10 pins on the first ball of a frame.   It is possible to score three strikes in the 10th frame because each bowler can throw a maximum of three balls in that frame.   A strike is scored as 10 pins plus the number of pins knocked down on the next two balls.   "Al threw a strike in each of the first five frames."

Strike Out – Throwing three strikes in the 10th frame.   "If Louie could strike out in the 10th frame, we could win this game."

Tap – When a pin or pins remain standing on what appeared to be a perfect hit into the 1-3 or 1-2 pockets.   Pins usually associated with taps include the 10 and 7 pins, while many bowlers say a true strike tap is for right handed bowlers to leave an 8 pin, and for left handed bowlers to leave a 9 pin. "A tap on the 8 pin on the 12th ball cost Dan a 300 game."

Timing – Coordination of all elements of delivery. Many associate timing with when the ball is released and overall smoothness of delivery. "Great timing and great bowling seem to go together."

Topping – Releasing the ball with fingers and thumb on top of the ball. A topped ball usually has poor revolutions and little striking power. "You need to get under the ball if you want to stop topping it."

Track – Referred to as the line the ball follows on the way to the pins. Some bowlers refer to the track as a line near the pins with little oil, while others call a track a line near the pins with a lot of oil. A track could be described as a "path" to the pins. "Let the ball hit the track." The oil line left on a ball is also called the track.

Turkey – Hitting three strikes in a row. "The 10th frame is a great time to go turkey shooting."

Washout – Leaving the 1-2-10 or 1-2-4-10 for right-handed bowlers, and the 1-3-7 or 1-3-6-7 for southpaws. Sometimes called a punch-out. "I hate to look down that lane and see a washout."

Web – Distance between the finger holes in a bowling ball. "What is the web on the ball?"

Weight Block -- The dense materials inside bowling balls designed to give the ball various rolling characteristics.

Weight Hole -- A hole drilled in a bowling ball to help achieve a specific static imbalance in the ball. It can not be larger than 1.25 inches in diameter, and is not used to grip the ball. "Ed likes a ball with a weight hole."

Wood – The bowling pins. "Despite that bad ball, he got a lot of wood."

BOWLING ASSOCIATIONS

•**Bowling Writers Association of America** was started in 1934 to support and promote better writing in the industry. Today, the mission of the association is "to create a continuing and new generation of media professionals dedicated to disseminating bowling history, news, features, and editorials while continuing its newly created scholarship program and long-standing programs honoring bowler performances and meritorious contributions. E-mail address is: webmaster@bowlingwriters.com. Web site: www.bowlingwriters.com.

•The **Federation of International des Quilleurs (FIQ)** was founded in 1952 to promote world interest in amateur tenpin and ninepin bowling. The FIQ, headquartered in Helsinki, Finland, is recognized by the International Olympic Committee as the world governing body for bowling.

•**The National Bowling Association** was formed in 1939 by African Americans and is open to all bowlers. TNBA lists 30,000 adult members, 7,500 junior members and sanctions 500 leagues. Address for TNBA is The National Bowling Association, Inc., 377 Park Avenue South - 7th Floor, New York, N.Y. 10016. Web address is http://www.tnbainc.org

•The **Professional Bowlers Association of America (PBA)** was founded in 1958 by the late Eddie Elias, an Akron, Ohio, attorney. In 2000 the PBA was purchased by former Microsoft executives Chris Peters, Mike Slade and Rob Glaser who turned the organization into a for-profit business. The PBA organizes, promotes and generally supervises all professional bowling activities. Web address is www.pbatour.com.

•The **United States Bowling Congress (USBC)** is the national governing body of bowling in the United States. The USBC establishes bowling rules, sanctions leagues and tournaments, maintains bowling records, issues bowling awards and generally assures that bowling lanes and equipment meet certain specifications to insure fairness in bowling.

The USBC was officially formed Jan. 1, 2005, when the American Bowling Congress (ABC), Women's International Bowling Congress (WIBC), Young American Bowling Alliance (YABA), and USA Bowling were merged into one organization of more than three million members. The ABC was formed in 1895, and the WIBC was formed in 1916.

Address for the USBC is United States Bowling Congress, 5301 S. 76th Street, Greendale, Wisc. 53129. Phone number is 1-800-514-2695.

Some other bowling and athletic associations include: Alabama State Bowling Association. Alabama Women's Bowling Association. American Wheelchair Bowling Association. Austin Bowling Association. Belgian Tenpin Bowling Federation. Barre-Montpelier Bowling Association. Bowling Proprietor's Association of New Jersey. British Tenpin Bowling Association. Brockton Bowling Association. Brothers Bowling Association. Buzzard Club of San Antonio. Calgary Chinese Bowling Association. Camden Burlington Mercer Tri-County Bowling Senate of the National Bowling Association. Canadian Lakehead Tenpin Bowling Association. Cecil-Hartford Counties Bowling Association. Central Alabama Bowling Association. Central Gippsland Tenpin Bowling Association. Chattahoochee Bowling Association. Chicago Metropolitan Bowling Association. Chinese Bowling Congress. Clearwater Women's Bowling Association. Colorado State Bowling Association. Colorado State Bowling Proprietors Association. Dallas Bowling Association. Decatur Women's Bowling Association. Endicott Bowling Association. European Bowling Proprietors Association. Family Bowling Organization. Fayetteville Bowling Association, Inc. Fort Wayne Bowling Association. Greater Atlanta YABA. Greater Calumet Area Bowling Association. Greater Cincinnati Bowling Association. Greater Birmingham Bowling Association. Greater Detroit Bowling Association. Greater Gainesville Bowling Association. Greater Hamilton Women's Bowling Association. Greater Peoria Bowling Association. Greater Pittsburgh Tenpin Bowling Association. Greater Miami Bowling Association. Greater Springfield, Ill., Bowling Association. Greenville Bowling Association. Huntsville Bowling Association. Huntsville Women's Bowling Association. Illinois Bowling Association. Illinois State Young American Bowling Alliance. International Association of Bowling Lane Specialists. International Gay Bowling Organization. Irish Tenpin Bowling Association. Kalamazoo Area Bowling. Kitsap County Bowling Association. Massachusetts Tri-County Bowling Association. Mexican-American Bowling Organization. Michigan State Bowling Association. Morris County Bowling Association. National Amateur Bowlers, Inc. National Collegiate Athletic Association. National Scholastic Athletic Association. Nation's Capital Area Bowling Association. New Orleans Women's Bowling Association. Northern Ireland Tenpin Bowling Federation. Orange County Bowling Association. Palomar Bowling Association. Paradise Bowling Association. Pennsylvania State Bowling Association. Portland Bowling Association. Rochester Bowling

Association. Rock Island Bowling Association. Rocket City Senate. San Fernando Valley Women's Bowling Association. San Jose Women's Bowling Association. Sharjah Filipino Bowling Club. Sigourney Bowling Association. Singapore Tenpin Bowling Congress. South Jersey Bowling Association. Southeast New Hampshire Bowling Association. Spokane Bowling Association. St. Petersburg Bowling Association Florida. Suncoast Bowling Association, Inc. Suncoast Women's Bowling Association. Tacoma Bowling. Tallahassee Bowling Association. Tennessee State YABA. Treasure Coast Bowling Association, Florida. Tri-City Bowling Association. Virginia State Bowling Association. Waukegan Women's Bowling Association. Windsor Essex Kent County Bowling Association. World Tenpin Bowling Association. York County Bowling Association.

BOWLING MUSEUM

The International Bowling Museum and Hall of Fame, 111 Stadium Plaza, St. Louis, Mo. 63102, is in downtown St. Louis near Busch Stadium. Phone number is: 314-231-6340. The museum is open from 11 a.m. to 4 p.m. Tuesday through Saturday October through March. From April through September it is open from 9 a.m. to 5 p.m. daily. Admission prices are: Adult $7.50. Senior (66+) $7. Youth (under 16) $6. Web Page: http//www.bowlingmuseum.com. *Note: Visitors may bowl on the Museum lanes.*

BOWLING STAR Walter Ray Williams Jr. signing autographs during a Regional tournament in 2005 at Lane Glo Lanes North in Port Richey, Fla. Williams freely gives autographs and poses for photos during his breaks.

BOWLING WEB SITES

Here are a few of the major bowling web sites on the Internet. The Internet has sites for just about every aspect of bowling. We have not tried to include all of the sites. Bowlers may find a variety of internet sites simply by selecting a search engine and typing in the word BOWLING.

•Bowling Proprietor's Association of America: www.BPAA.com
•Bowling Writers Association of America: www.bowlingwriters.com
•International Bowling Museum and Hall of Fame:
www.bowlingmuseum.com
•Pennsylvania State Bowling Association: www.psbabowl.org
•Professional Bowler's Association: www.PBA.com
•United States Bowling Congress: www.bowl.com

BOWLING WEB SITES (Equipment)
•AMF: www.AMF.com
•Brunswick: www.Columbia300.com
•Brunswick: www.Brunswickbowling.com
•Ebonite: www.Ebonite.com
•Hammer: www.Hammerbowling.com
•Storm: www.Stormbowling.com
•Track, Inc.: www.trackbowling.com
•Equipment: www.bowling.com
•Equipment: www.bowlingball.com
•Equipment: www.bowlingindex.com
•Equipment: www.bowlerstore.com
•Equipment: www.bowlersparadise.com
•Equipment: www.bowlerssupply.com
•Shoes: www.dynothane.com
•Shoes: www.dextershoe.com
BOWLING WEB SITES (General)
•www.hickoksports.com
•www.legendsbowling.com
•www.freep.com
•www.infoplease.com
•www.bowlingfans.com
•www.amug.org

BOWLING PERIODICALS

Here is a list and a brief description of some of the periodicals available in which the main subject is tenpin bowling:

•***Bowling Digest*** magazine is published four times a year. Its content includes bowling instruction, bowler profiles, interviews and coverage of professional bowling, USBC and international competition. The magazine was started in 1983. It is published by the Century Publishing Co., 990 Grove St., Evanston, IL. 60201-4370. Phone: 847-491-6440. Web site: www.centurysports.net.

•***Bowlers Journal International*** is a monthly publication started in 1913. It covers all aspects of bowling and is especially focused on interviews, data and technical aspects of bowling. It is owned by Luby Publishing, Inc., 122 S. Michigan Ave., Suite 1506, Chicago, IL 60603. Phone 312-341-1110. Web site: www.bowlersjournal.com. E-mail: email@bowlersjournal.com.

•***Bowling Proprietor*** was started in 1954. It is a monthly magazine that features information updating lane owners on trends and developments in that field. It is published by the Bowling Proprietor's Association of America, P.O. Box 5802, Arlington, TX. Phone: 817-649-5105.

•***Bowling This Month*** bills the magazine as a publication for those who are serious about bowling. Subjects covered include technique, lane play, mental conditioning, bowling ball comparisons, ball motion and equipment reviews. Address is P.O. Box 966, San Marcos, Texas, 78667. Phone: 800-282-7043 or 512-353-8906. Web site: www.bowlingthismonth.com.

•***Bowling World*** is a monthly newspaper covering news of interest to bowlers and the bowling industry. Subscription rate is $25 a year. Mailing address is P.O. Box 111178, Campbell, CA. 95011-1178. Phone: 408-621-7332. E-mail: readit@bowlingworld.com. Web site: www.bowlingworld.com.

•***US Bowler*** is a publication of the United States Bowling Congress, 5301 S. 76th St., Greendale, Wisc., 53129. It is published quarterly and mailed to USBC members. The magazine features bowling advice from the nation's best bowlers, USBC news and tournament coverage. Telephone is 414-421-6400. E-mail address is USBowler@bowl.com.

BOWLING BOOKS & VIDEOS

There have been a number of books written about bowling over the past 70 years. Most are how-to books written by leading bowlers and bowling coaches. Here are just a few of the books -- we have more information on some than others -- you might look at to help improve your game or simply learn more about tenpin bowling:

•***Winning Bowling*** by Earl Anthony with Dawson Taylor is a guide to bowling techniques. It was published in 1977 by Contemporary Books, Inc., Chicago. ISBN 0-8092-7792-1.
The late Earl Anthony won 41 Profes-
sional Bowling Association tour championships. Dawson Taylor, sports-
writer and a 200-average bowler, had
written 23 books at the time of *Winning Bowling.*

•***Bowling 300*** by Dan Herbst.
Published in 1993, *Bowling 300* fea-
tures PBA stars Walter Ray Williams
Jr., Mark Baker, Marc McDowell and
Bob Benoit sharing their bowling techniques. Contemporary Books, Inc., Chicago. Herbst, a sports writer specializing in bowling and soccer, wrote for many publications, authored several books and contributed to several books. He died in 2001 at the age of 48. ISBN: 0-8092-3823-3.

•***Bowling 200+*** by Mike Aulby was published in 1989 by Contem-
porary Books, Inc., Chicago. The book features Mike Aulby's tips on how to bowl better. Aulby, Indianapolis, Ind., was elected to the USBC and PBA bowling halls of fame and was the Bowling Writer's bowler of the year in 1985, 1989 and 1995. Motorbooks.com. Printed in China. ISBN: 0-8092-4338-5.

•***Bowling: Knowledge is the Key*** by Fred Borden. Lessons from one of bowling's most famous coaches. Offers fundamentals and advanced concepts in bowling. Published in May, 1986, by Bowling Green State University. ISBN: 0-9619-1770-9. Borden is a former coach of Team USA.

•***Bowling Execution*** by John Jowdy was published in 2002. It is a bowling improvement book. Jowdy is a Hall of Fame coach who has tu-
tored many top professional bowlers. Human Kinetics.
www.HumanKinetics.com. Printed in the U.S. ISBN: 0-7360-4217-2.

•***Bowling for Beginners: Simple Steps to Strikes & Spares*** by Don Nace. Features simple steps to strikes and spares. Full-color photos by Bruce Curtis. For bowlers ages 9-12. Published in June, 2001, by Sterling Publishing Co. ISBN: 0-8069-4968-6.

•***Bowling Fundamentals*** by Michael Mullen offers lesson in bowling basics. It was published in 2004 by Publication Champaign, IL: Human Information: Kinetics. ISBN: 0-7360-5120-1.

•***Better Bowling**** by Joe Wilman. Published in 1953 by A.S. Barnes and Co., New York, N.Y., it is old but still offers solid information from one of the game's smoothest and best all-time bowlers. Lots of drawings and photos. Wilman was elected to the Bowling Hall of Fame in 1951.

•***Bowling*** by Patty Costello with Alfred Glossbrenner. Published in 1977. Costello, Scranton, Pa., was Professional Bowler of the Year in 1972, 1976 and 1985. One of the nation's most popular bowlers, she is a member of the Women's International Bowling Congress Hall of Fame.

•***Bowling: Steps to Success*** by Robert H. Stirckland features drills to develop bowlers' skills and techniques at their own pace. Lots of illustrations. Strickland is a bowling coach.

•***Bowl Like A Pro*** by David Ozio with Dan Herbst. Published in 1992. Ozio, Vidor, Texas, was the Bowling Writer's bowler of the year in 1991 and was elected to the PBA Hall of Fame in 1995.

•***Bowling Basics*** by Chuck Pezzano was published in 1984 by Prentice-Hall. It has illustrations by Bill Gow and a lot of photos by Arvid Knudsen. ISBN: 0-1308-0516-0.

•***Par Bowling, The Challenge*** by Thomas Kouros. First published in 1976, this book is one of the most extensive, in-depth bowling instruction volumes ever written. Kouros, associated with bowling more than 50 years, was a bowling instructor at the University of Illinois and DePaul University, owner of a bowling center, cofounder of Chicago's Paddock Traveling Classic League, member of the 1952-1953 DePaul University Midwest Intercollegiate championship team, and holder of three 300 games and a high series of 812.

•***From Gutterballs to Strikes*** by Mike Durbin and Dan Herbst. Durbin, three-time winner of the Tournament of Champions, member of the PBA Hall of Fame and a commentator for ESPN, offers ways to overcome bowling's 101 most common errors. Focuses on how to correct bowling mistakes. Published by McGraw Hill in January, 1998. ISBN: 0-8092-3058-5.

•***Complete Guide to Bowling Strikes Vol. 2*** by George Richard Allen.

•***Bowler's Start-up: A Beginner's Guide to Bowling*** by Doug Werner. Published in 1995.

•***Bowlers Guide***, a bowling textbook with Dick Ritger and Judy Soutar. Features sections for juniors, seniors and lefthanders. Lots of bowling tips.

•***Focused for Bowling*** by Dean R. Hinitz and Brian Voss. Published in October, 2002. Voss was elected to the PBA Hall of Fame in 1994.

•***Bowling: How to Master the Game*** by Parker Bohn III and Dan Herbst. Bohn, 1999 Professional Bowlers Association Player of the Year, talks about all aspects of championship-caliber bowling. Contributors include Mike Aulby, Chris Barnes, Cindy Coburn-Carroll, Johnny Petraglia, Mark Roth, Kim Terrell and Tammy Turner. Published by Universe Publishing in 2000. ISBN: 0-7893-0494-5.

•***Right Down Your Alley: The Beginners Book of Bowling*** by Vesma Grinfelds and Bonnie Hultstrand.

•***Bowling Strikes*** by Dawson Taylor. Aimed at bowlers with averages under 200.

•***Essential Bowling*** by Michael Benson.

•***The Ultimate Guide to Weight Training for Bowling*** by Robert Price.

•***The Pro Approach*** by Larry Matthews. Matthews is a professional bowler, bowling coach and bowling writer.

•***The Science of Bowling Maintenance 2000*** by Remo N. Picchietti. Book is for bowling center operators. Picchietti is president of DBA Products Co.

•***A Roll Down Memory Lane*** by Gideon Bosker and Bianca Lencek-Bosker. Chronicle Books, San Francisco, Calif.

•***The Profitable Pro Shop*** by Larry Lichstein with Bob and Jim Schumaker. This book is regarded as a pro shop owner's bible. Covers everything from display and drilling to dealing with customers. Old but good. Published in 1985 by Stone Walled Press, San Jose, Calif. Lichstein, member of the PBA at age 18, was inducted into the PBA Hall of Fame Meritorious Service section in 1996. As player service director for the PBA, Lichstein followed the PBA tour for more than 20 years with a "rolling pro shop." He is still known as the ball driller of the pros. He operates three pro shops in Fort Myers, Fla.

•***Bill Taylor's Fitting and Drilling A Bowling Ball.*** One of the best old time books on how to properly drill bowling balls for specific bowling styles.

VIDEOS

•***Secrets to Better Bowling*** with Walter Ray Williams Jr. Covers bowling improvement for all skill levels, discusses lane conditions, spare shooting techniques, practice routines and more. Williams, Ocala, Fla., is a member of the USBC and PBA bowling halls of fame.

•***The Feelings of Bowling*** - Vol. I, Vol .II, Vol. III with Dick Ritger. Covers hooks, line bowling and release. Volume III was produced in 1996. Ritger, elected to the PBA Hall of Fame in 1978, is known for his teaching skill and holder of 20 PBA titles.

•***Bowl Your Best Game*** with Earl Anthony, Dick Weber, Mike Aulby and Leila Wagner. All-time bowling greats teach bowling.

•***A Pro's Guide to Better Bowling*** - Vol. I, Vol. II with Don Johnson, Akron, Ohio. Produced in the 1980s.   Johnson, elected to the USBC and PBA bowling halls of fame, was the Bowling Writer's bowler of the year in 1971 and 1972.

•***Bowling for Women Only*** with Anne Marie Duggan, 15-time PWBA champion; Fred Borden, noted coach and USA Team coach from 1986 through 1996; Jeri Edwards, pro bowler and 1990-1996 Team USA coach, and Pat Duggan, USBC certified coach. Issued in 1999, the video is presented by Ebonite, Storm, Dexter and Master.

•***Maximum Bowling*** with Marshall Holman. He demonstrates the five-point program designed by bowling coach John Jowdy. Covers rhythm, slide, hand position, release point and angle, and follow-through. Holman,

Medford, Ore., was bowler of the year in 1987 and inducted into the PBA Hall of Fame in 1990.

•***Going for 300*** by Earl Anthony. Offers an analysis of wrist, arm, body and foot positions, ways to handle lane conditions and techniques to improve and keep a higher average.

•***Bowling Fun and Fundamentals for Boys and Girls*** with coaches Fred Borden and Ken Yokobosky teach young bowlers all they need to know to excel in bowling. Topics covered include rules and etiquette, equipment, approach, arm swing, release, follow-through, common faults and practice methods. (DVD).

•***Essential Keys to Better Bowling*** with coaches Fred Borden and Ken Yokobosky covers equipment, delivery, the strike ball, making spares, lane conditions, mental game and more. (DVD).

•***Perfect Form*** with Marshall Holman and Johnny Petraglia. The Hall of Fame bowlers demonstrate through body positioning exact skills needed in bowling. The video features slow-motion sequences and computer-enhanced pictures. Holman and Petraglia are members of the PBA Bowling Hall of Fame.

•***Lets Bowl with Dick Weber.*** Dick Weber was one of the all-time bowling greats. He was elected to USBC Bowling Hall of Fame in 1970, and to the PBA Bowling Hall of Fame in 1975.

•***Ball Drilling & Fitting.*** Dave Smart, Team Columbia representative, shows techniques for proper ball drilling and fitting. This video is geared to the pro-shop folks and those interested in knowing more about bowling ball preparation. Produced in 1994.

Fast Facts

Youngest: Michael Tang of San Francisco became the youngest bowler to record a sanctioned 300 game March 11, 2006, when he hit the perfect score in the Daly City All Stars Scratch Trios League in Sea Bowl, Pacifica, Calif. He was 10 years, three months and 16 days old.   He hit 163 and 193 after the 300 for a 656 series.

Tang was three months younger than the previous record holder, Josey LaRocco of Louisville, Ky. LaRocco bowled a perfect game Feb. 14, 1998.

Hurst Bowling Supplies of Luzerne, Pa., posted a 3,868 team series Feb. 23, 1994. Team members were Brian Snear, Carmen Marsit, Bob Buckery, Howard Holly, Jeff Piatt and non-playing captain Charlie Hurst.

THIS DATE IN BOWLING

January 1 -- The **United States Bowling Congress** (USBC) was officially formed in 2005 merging and replacing the American Bowling Congress (ABC), Women's International Bowling Congress (WIBC) and the Young American Bowling Alliance (YABA).

January 20 -- **Brent Arecement**, Kenner, La., rolled an 888 three-game total in 1990 to set the record in that category for male youths. That record was broken Dec. 3, 2005, when **Robert Mushtare,** 17, hit a 900 at Fort Drum, N.Y.

January 23 -- **Emily Snyder**, Whitehall, Pa., hit a three-game total of 843 in 2000 to set a record in that category for female youths.

February 1 -- **Donna "Mighty Mite" Adamek** was born in 1957 in Duarte, Calif. Woman Bowler of the Year from 1978 through 1981, she won five major championships during that period. She is a member of the Professional Women's Hall of Fame and the Women's International Bowling Congress Hall of Fame.

February 2 -- **Jeremy Sonnenfeld** of Lincoln, Neb., rolled the first sanctioned 900 series in bowling history in 1997. That broke **Tom Jordan's** record of 899.

February 13 -- **Lonnie Billiter Jr.** rolled the all-time ninth sanctioned 900 series in 2006 in Fairfield, Ohio.

February 15 -- The **O.T. Hills** men's team of St. Charles, Mo., broke the single game team record in 2001 with a total of 1,413, an average of 282.6 per man.

February 19 -- **Robert Mushtare**, 17-year-old from Carthage, N.Y., became the first bowler ever to record two 900 series when he hit the magic scores while pre-bowling for the Pine Plains Junior/Senior League at the Pine Plains Bowling Center in Fort Drum, N.Y., in 2006. He recorded his first 900 Dec. 3, 2005, at the same lanes. The USBC sanctioned the scores June 19, 2006.

February 23 -- **Hurst Bowling Supplies** of Luzerne, Pa., set a new team series record in 1994 with a 3,868 total to break the 1958 record of 3,858 set by the famous Budweiser team of St. Louis.

March 7 -- **Tom Jordan** broke **Allie Brandt's** 50-year-old series record of

886 with an 899 series in Union, N.J., in 1989.

March 14 -- The **Contour Power Grips** five member women's team of West Bloomfield, Mich, set the all-time team single-game record with a 1,318 in 1998. That is an average of 262.2 per bowler.

March 25 -- **Mike Aulby**, PBA and USBC Hall of Fame member, was born in 1960 in Indianapolis, Ind. Aulby, winner of 25 professional bowling championships, was named bowler of the decade for the 1980s. **Norm Duke**, Hall of Fame member, was born in 1964.

April 1 -- The **Limo Exchange** five-man team of New Castle, Del., broke the all-time team total record in 2004 with a score of 3,934. That is an average of 1,311 per game and 786.8 per man.

April 11 -- Hall of Fame bowler **Joe Joseph** was born in 1918. He died June 10, 1988.

April 13 -- **George Billick** was born in 1910 in Old Forge, Pa. He was the first to bowl more than 15 sanctioned perfect games. He died Sept. 8, 1992. He was inducted into the USBC Hall of Fame in 1982.

April 22 -- **Mark Wukoman** posted the lastest 900 series, the 11th sanctioned, in Greenfield, Wisc., in 2006.

April 28 -- **Earl Anthony**, winner of 41 Professional Bowling Association championships, was born in 1938 in Cornelius, Ore. He died Aug. 14, 2001.

May 2 -- **James Hylton**, Salem, Ore., rolled the fifth sanctioned 900 series in 2001.

June 12 -- **Jeff K. Campbell II** recorded the sixth 900 series in bowling history in New Castle, Pa., in 2004.

July 22 -- **Floretta "Doty" McCutcheon** was born in Ottumwa, Ia., in 1888. She rolled her first game, a 69, in 1923 at the age of 35. In 1930 she toured the U.S., bowling 10 perfect games, 11 three-game 800s, and more than a hundred 700 series. Through her tours and School of Bowling in New York and Chicago, she is credited with introducing some 250,000 people to the sport. She retired in 1939 after registering a sanctioned 206 league average which stood as the record for 35 years.

July 25 -- ABC and PBA Hall of Fame member **Billy Hardwick** was born in 1941 in Florence, Ala. He retired after the 1976 season with 17 professional tournament wins. He operates a bowling center in Memphis, Tenn.

July 29 -- Hall of Fame bowler **Don Carter** was born in 1926. He was named Bowler of the Year six times by the Bowling Writer's Association of America. In 1970 he was voted Greatest of All-Time by the BWAA.

August 9 -- **Chris Lucas**, Bonesteel, S.D., ended his record-setting streak of 164 consecutive 600 series in one league in 2005. The streak began Nov. 16, 2001. The old record of 129 straight 600 series was held by **Jim Hoster** of Wayne, N.J. He ended his streak in 1998.

August 10 -- Jackie Mitskavich, Van Wert, Ohio, broke the all-time women's three-game series record when she hit 877 in 1997. The record was broken by **Karen Rosenburg** in 2001 with an 878 in Rolla, Mo.

September 5 -- The **American Bowling Congress** was organized in New York City in 1895.

September 11 -- Chris Schenkel, announcer for ABC-TV's Pro Bowlers Tour telecasts from 1962 until 1997, died in 2005 at the age of 82.

September 27 -- Buddy Bomar was born in Chicago in 1916. Holder of many championships, he was one of the main promoters of bowling as he conducted clinics across the U.S. as a member of the Brunswick exhibition staff. He died Nov. 17, 1989.

September 29 -- Vince Wood, Moreno Valley, Calif., hit the third sanctioned 900 series in 1999.

October 6 -- Hall of Fame bowler **Walter Ray Williams Jr.** was born in Eureka, Calif., in 1959. He joined the Professional Bowling Association in 1980 at the age of 21. He won his 41st tour championship in 2006, tieing **Earl Anthony** for most professional wins.

October 25 -- In 1939 **Allie Brandt** rolled an 886 series in Lockport, N.Y., on games of 297, 289 and 300. He weighed just 122 pounds.

November 9 --Tony Raventini, Milwaukee, Wisc., rolled the second sanctioned 900 series in 1998.

November 20 -- The **All-Star Grill** five-member women's team of Livonia, Mich, set a new team series record of 3,600 in 2000. That's an average of 720 per bowler.

December 9 -- Darren Pomije hit the seventh sanctioned 900 series in bowling history in New Prague, Minn., in 2004.

December 12 -- Karen Rosenburg, 37, rolled the highest three-game total in women's bowling history when she hit an 878 at the Coachlite Lanes in Rolla, Mo., on games of 299, 279 and 300 in 2001.

December 14 -- Allie Brandt was born in 1902 in Lockport, N.Y. He rolled an 886 on games of 297, 289 and 300 on Oct. 25, 1939.

December 23 -- Hall of Fame bowler **Dick Weber** was born in Indianapolis, Ind., in 1929. He died Feb. 13, 2005, in St. Louis, Mo.

December 28 -- Robby Portalatin, Jackson, Mich., hit the fourth sanctioned 900 series in 2000.

PINBOYS working the four lanes of St. John's Recreation Bowling Lanes in Susquehanna, Pa., in 1966. Pinboys stacked the 3.5-pound pins in the machines and lowered the rack to set them on the deck. The pin-setting machines were an improvement over when pin setters hand sat (two pins per hand) the pins on pegs raised from below the deck by a foot lever. The ball was returned with the help of gravity on the rails between each set of lanes. Pinboys in the 1950s and 1960s earned between $1.10 to $1.50 a lane for three league games. Despite the dangers, it was unusual for a pin boy to get hit by a flying pin. *(Photo by William S. Young)*

HANDICAPS		80% OF 210					
Bowler's Handbook							
Avg.	Handicap	Avg.	Handicap	Avg.	Handicap	Avg.	Handicap
210	0	179	24	148	49	117	74
209	0	178	25	147	50	116	75
208	1	177	26	146	51	115	76
207	2	176	27	145	52	114	76
206	3	175	28	144	52	113	77
205	4	174	28	143	53	112	78
204	4	173	29	142	54	111	79
203	5	172	30	141	55	110	80
202	6	171	31	140	56	109	80
201	7	170	32	139	56	108	81
200	8	169	32	138	57	107	82
199	8	168	33	137	58	106	83
198	9	167	34	136	59	105	84
197	10	166	35	135	60	104	84
196	11	165	36	134	60	103	85
195	12	164	36	133	61	102	86
194	12	163	37	132	62	101	87
193	13	162	38	131	63	100	88
192	14	161	39	130	64	99	88
191	15	160	40	129	64	98	89
190	16	159	40	128	65	97	90
189	16	158	41	127	66	96	91
188	17	157	42	126	67	95	92
187	18	156	43	125	68	94	92
186	19	155	44	124	68	93	93
185	20	154	44	123	69	92	94
184	20	153	45	122	70	91	95
183	21	152	46	121	71	90	96
182	22	151	47	120	72	89	96
181	23	150	48	119	72	88	97
180	24	149	48	118	73	87	98

See Page 72 for an explanation of how to figure handicaps.

Best of the Century

Bowling Magazine in 1999 named its 20 greatest male bowlers of the 20th Century. While a number of bowlers are not on the list who might be, it's easy to agree with the magazine's three unanimous choices: Dick Weber, winner of professional bowling titles in five decades; Don Carter, six-time Bowler of the Year, and Earl Anthony, winner of 41 PBA titles.

Others on the list are Mike Aulby, Nelson Burton Jr., Ned Day, Billy Hardwick, Marshall Holman, Don Johnson, Bill Lillard, Hank Marino, Junie McMahon, Joe Norris, Dick Ritger, Mark Roth, Carmen Salvino, Harry Smith, Andy Varipapa, Pete Weber and Walter Ray Williams Jr.

| HANDICAPS | | 90% OF 210 | | | | | |
Bowler's Handbook							
Avg.	Handicap	Avg.	Handicap	Avg.	Handicap	Avg.	Handicap
210	0	179	28	148	56	117	84
209	1	178	29	147	57	116	85
208	2	177	30	146	58	115	86
207	3	176	31	145	59	114	86
206	4	175	32	144	60	113	87
205	5	174	32	143	60	112	88
204	5	173	33	142	61	111	89
203	6	172	34	141	62	110	90
202	7	171	35	140	63	109	91
201	8	170	36	139	64	108	92
200	9	169	37	138	65	107	93
199	10	168	38	137	66	106	94
198	11	167	39	136	67	105	95
197	12	166	40	135	68	104	96
196	13	165	41	134	68	103	96
195	14	164	41	133	69	102	97
194	14	163	42	132	70	101	98
193	15	162	43	131	71	100	99
192	16	161	44	130	72	99	100
191	17	160	45	129	73	98	101
190	18	159	46	128	74	97	102
189	19	158	47	127	75	96	103
188	20	157	48	126	76	95	104
187	21	156	49	125	77	94	104
186	22	155	50	124	77	93	105
185	23	154	50	123	78	92	106
184	23	153	51	122	79	91	107
183	24	152	52	121	80	90	108
182	25	151	53	120	81	89	109
181	26	150	54	119	82	88	109
180	27	149	55	118	83	87	110

See Page 72 for an explanation of how to figure handicaps.

Detroit's Eddie Lubanski

Eddie Lubanski, Detroit, Mich., earned as much as $50,000 a year at the height of his bowling career in the 1950s when the average income was $5,500 a year and gasoline was 30 cents a gallon. In 1959 he bowled consecutive 300 games in Miami while becoming only the second man to win four ABC titles in a single tournament.

Lubanski also was a member of BPAA championship teams in 1952, 1953, 1954 and 1964. He held the highest lifetime average record with a 204 for more than 25 years. He was inducted into the Bowling Hall of Fame in 1971.

OTHER BOWLING GAMES

• **Ninepin** is the forerunner of 10-pin bowling and its play is limited to primarily around the south-Texas, San Antonio areas in the U.S.   Highest score results in ninepin bowling by knocking down all pins except the large number 5-pin in the center of a diamond layout. The World Ninepin Association, a branch of the Federation of International des Quilleurs (FIQ), governs ninepin bowling. Standard 10-pin bowling balls are used.

• **Five-pin** was invented by a man named Thomas Ryan in 1908. He was looking for a game for the upper class that did not participate in 10-pin bowling. Duckpins were first used, and then later modified when a heavy rubber band was added around the middle of the pin. Today the game is played with the duckpin ball and a possible high score is 450 because the head pin is worth five points, the two adjacent pins are worth three points each, and the back two pins are worth two points each. The game is played mostly in Canada. Its governing organization is the Manitoba Five Pin Bowling Association, Second Floor, 200 Main Street, Winnipeg, Manitoba, R3C 4M2.

• **Candlepin** bowling, founded in Worcester, Mass., is played in the western New England states and in Canada's Maritime Provinces. Candlepins today are 15.75 inches high with 2 15/16-inch centers that taper to 1.75 inches on each end. Scoring is the same as in 10-pin bowling, except bowlers are allowed three balls per frame to knock down all the pins. Candlepin balls are 4.5 inches in diameter and weigh no more that 2 pounds 7 ounces. While a 300-game is possible, the highest sanctioned score in the sport is a 240. Candlepin Bowling is governed by the International Candlepin Bowling Association, 3 Arrowhead Drive, Bow, N.H. 03304.

• **Duckpin** bowling was born in Baltimore in 1900 as a summertime novelty, but for many years competed with 10-pin bowling as the favorite sport. Duckpins are bowled on 10-pin size lanes using balls that are five inches in diameter and weighing three pounds 12 ounces, with 10 pins of 9 and 13/32 high and 2.25 inches in diameter set in a triangle shape 12 inches apart. Bowlers get three balls per frame to knock down all the pins. Today, duckpin bowling is played almost exclusively in the Baltimore-Washington area. Its governing body is the National Duckpin Bowling Congress, 4991 Fairview Ave., Linthicum, MD. 21090. E-mail: NationalDuckpin@aol.com

SUGGESTIONS

Do you have suggestions to help make Bowler's Handbook better? If so, just send them to Bowler's Handbook, McIntosh Publishing, Inc., P.O. Box 934, Elfers, FL. 34680-0934. McIntoshPublishing@Yahoo.com

INDEX

Fast Facts

Joe Wilman once held 16 American Bowling Congress records. In 1953 he composed the book "Better Bowling" for the Barnes Sports Library series.

Fast Facts

•**Eddie Elias,** Akron, Ohio, attorney, founded the Professional Bowlers Association in 1958. Elias died in Naples, Fla., Nov. 15, 1998, at age 69. The PBA was purchased in 2000 by former Microsoft executives Chris Peters, Miker Slade and Rob Glaser.

•**Lou Campi** was a great pro bowler despite the fact he slid on the wrong foot. He was nicknamed "Wrong Foot" Lou.

THE AUTHOR

Bowler's Handbook was written, compiled and designed by Ron McIntosh, bowler, journalist, publisher, adjunct speech instructor at Pasco-Hernando Community College, New Port Richey, Fla., and former communication instructor and newspaper advisor at Independence Community College in Independence, Kansas.

"My mom loved bowling, and she began teaching me to bowl when I was nine years old. I became so involved I got a job as a foul-line watcher and pin boy at the four-lane bowling center in my hometown, Susquehanna, Pa. Those years became the foundation for my lifelong love of the game and curiosity about bowling and the bowlers who love America's number one participant sport."

McIntosh holds a BA from Empire State College, Rochester, N.Y., and a MA from Pittsburg State University, Pittsburg, Kansas. He resides and bowls in New Port Richey.

Ron McIntosh

Thanks to all those who helped put this book together.

They include: My wife, editor-in-chief and counselor, Paulett. My daughters and listeners, Lori, Kathleen and Coleen. My neighbor and bowling buddy, Gary Giessel. My bowling teachers, Mike Allan and Don Wilmarth. My motivator, Karen Roush. The computer guy, Bill Manuel. My bowling friends in these pages, Kansas, Pennsylvania and Florida.

The folks in Susquehanna who showed a lad the special friendships, relationships and sportsmanship in bowling. Some of those were Leo Spoonhour, Lou Parrillo, Jack Barry, Stub Card, Blackie Sellitto, Jess Richards, Bob Furkay, George Napolitano, Mary Tuttle, Alice Spoonhour and U.G. Baker.

And my Mom, Veda, who taught me to love the game.